WHY GOD WAITS FOR YOU TO PRAY

Thomas Keith Roberts

PRESS

DEDICATION

To my parents
J.L. and Myrtle Roberts
Who brought me up "in the training and
instruction of the Lord."

CONTENTS

PREFACE

As you read this, be aware that many have influenced my understanding of prayer and have also played a part in this book. Some of them I will mention, but so many have influenced me that I can't refer to them all. Just know that you are appreciated and loved in the Lord.

Thanks to Albert and Patsy Lemmons for their mentoring and encouragement toward the serious prayer life for many years.

Thanks also to Hugh and Jo Gower along with Carl and Monica Johnson for their help in proofreading and editing and their encouragement.

To Dave and Kim Butts of Harvest Prayer Ministries for their warm Christian fellowship and their encouragement as we work together to see that Jesus' church becomes a house of prayer.

To my wife Judy, who is always faithful, always cares and always devotes herself to serving His church. Thanks for your undying love and support.

Thanks also to our children: Kevin, Angela & Mike, Hannah and Jenna for the bright glow you bring to life. May God continue to richly bless.

Also thanks to Darrell and Lana Frazier who encouraged me years ago to write this book.

Thanks to the White's Ferry Road Church of Christ and the School of Biblical Studies, who encouraged me and shaped me into the disciple I am today.

And thanks to the Calhoun Church of Christ for putting up with my preaching for nearly three decades. I appreciate your love and support. And thanks for being a big-hearted church willing to launch out and learn more about prayer.

Also, there are several writers who've mentored me in prayer: E.M. Bounds, S.D. Gordon, C. Peter Wagner, R.A. Torrey, Watchman Nee, Richard Foster, Dick Eastman and many others. If you're aware of their writings, you'll see their influence in this book.

-Keith Roberts 2007

INTRODUCTION

Aviation pioneer Handley Page didn't like it, but he had to fly into a remote area and land. His landing went fine, so did the takeoff... but then it happened.

He heard gnawing. It must be a rat, probably a huge jungle rat!

Page's stomach sank as he thought about how much damage a gnawing rat could do to delicate aviation systems. And in these remote areas, repair facilities and mechanics didn't exist. Something had to be done, but he had no co-pilot to spell him while he chased a rat throughout the plane.

Just then he remembered that rats can't live at high altitude. So he pulled back on the stick and began to climb. Higher the plane soared, until Page found it hard to breathe.

Gasping for breath, he listened. The gnawing stopped. He didn't hear it again, so he hoped for the best and waited to land.

At his next stop, sure enough, Handley Page found a dead rat behind his cockpit.

Like Page, believers today seem distracted - infested by the rats of secularism, busyness, materialism, worry, religious controversies - well, you can probably list them better than I can.

It's clear that God's people today need a break from the rat race.

So why not soar higher? This soaring, higher flight into a single-hearted pursuit of God can't help but choke out the rats.

That's what this book is about. Not just learning to pray, but learning to soar. And learning to come awake to the startling fact that God *waits* for us to pray. Even heaven itself waits for God's people to decide to soar higher.

Is God really waiting for you to pray? The ball might just be in your court...

Chapter One: DID JESUS BELIEVE IT?

"During the days of Jesus' life on earth, he offered up prayers and petitions with loud cries and tears to the one who could save him from death, and he was heard because of his reverent submission." (Hebrews 5:7 NIV)

When Heaven Opened

Did Jesus himself believe that one *must* pray before God would intervene?

Was *his* prayer life proactive?

Was prayer at the top of his priority list? Did things change when Jesus prayed?

If you don't think Jesus believed that the Father waits for us to pray, *investigate his approach to prayer*:

When Jesus prayed, heaven opened. It had no choice.

When Jesus prayed, demons scattered. God's angels flew faster. Supernatural strongholds swayed and crashed. Hearts melted. Thousands ate from one little boy's lunch. The blind saw. The deaf heard.

When Jesus prayed, the sea became a liquid sidewalk. Moses and Elijah reported for a mountain top conference. The dead shrugged off their tombs and hugged their relatives.

When Jesus prayed, people knew *something* would happen!

When Jesus prayed, his disciples rubbed goose bumps as they listened; the hair on their necks stood at attention. They listened with that uncomfortable reverence that surrounds an eternity moment (like a deathbed), that eerie feeling that the unseen is at your elbow, that the supernatural hovers just out of sight.

When Jesus prayed, the supernatural became natural... almost normal. His prayers hit like nuclear warheads while his disciples played with firecrackers.

When Jesus prayed, heaven opened... and listened.

When Jesus prayed, angels strengthened him during his Gethsemane agony. He prayed, and then embraced the thorns, the cold spikes, the bloody cross.

When Jesus prayed, neither heaven nor earth were the same.

When Jesus prayed "Father, forgive them" he struck a deathblow to Satan's grip on man. The devil's dark kingdom hasn't recovered yet. It won't.

When Jesus prayed, heaven opened.

Why? What was it? What was there in his prayers that brought heaven to earth?

For one thing, he knew how heaven works. It was his homeland. He came from there to here. Like a traveler from a foreign land, he knew the customs, language and protocol of home.

Prayer was his native tongue. He knew how to pray, what to pray and when to pray. He knew the most advanced tactics of spiritual warfare. He was, and *is,* the undisputed World Champion, The Master, and Ultimate Warrior of prayer.

Certainly Jesus could pray with awesome, staggering power. But it goes further than that.

He's actually the embodiment of prayer.

He Embodied Prayer

Think of it this way: Imagine a seasoned safari guide leads his band of tourists deep into the jungle. For days they trek into the wilderness enjoying the adventure.

When the time comes to head back, the safari guide gathers his group for the return to civilization. He explains the return procedure, yet one tourist questions his plan.

"I don't think that's the right way. Are you sure that way will lead us back?"

The safari guide smiles. He ignores the tenderfoot's comment, launching back into his presentation.

The man speaks up again, "I don't think that's the way back. I think it's the path over there. I believe we ought to go *that* way."

With a confident stare the safari guide replies, "Listen, I've lived here all my life. I've led safaris here for thirty years. Technically, you people are *lost*. As far as you're concerned, I *am the way...* now follow *me!*" They follow.

Jesus not only *knows* the way, he *is* the way. He not only knows how one must be saved, he *is* our salvation. He not only knows God, he *is* God. And he not only knows how to pray, he *is* prayer. He's the embodiment of prayer itself.

In fact Psalm 109:4 describes the Messiah by saying, "I am prayer" (original Hebrew.) That Psalm predicts the coming Messiah and says he *is* prayer. Just as he is light, the Bread of Life and the resurrection... he *is* prayer.

While on earth, his 100% devotion to prayer staggered his disciples and scattered his enemies. He stated his own devotion to his Father (and to prayer) in these words: "I tell you the truth, the Son can do nothing by himself... By myself I can do nothing; I judge only as I hear... for I seek not to please myself but him who sent me." (John 5:19, 30 NIV)

How could he exercise such total devotion to his Father without the posture of prayer? The intensity of Jesus' relationship with his Father demanded it, for *without prayer there is no personal fellowship between God and man.* That's why the Psalmist quotes Messiah as saying, "I am prayer."

Jesus was, and is, the embodiment of praying mankind.

Prayer Before Adam

And here's another way he *is* prayer; his prayer life spans eternity.

Communion with God fills heaven. That's the nature of it. Heaven's landscape is filled with the Divine conversation like a loving home echoing with family conversation. You can't have a true heaven without communion with God, so *you can't even imagine heaven without "prayer" being a feature of it.*

When God said "Let *us* make man in *our* image", that's an example of Divine communion (or conversation) within the Godhead. (Genesis 1:26 NIV) Or when Jesus is called the "Lamb that was slain from the creation of the world" (Revelation 13:8 NIV) – there you have communication within the Divine Mind about Jesus' sacrifice before Adam was ever created.

The same is true when God said he "chose us in him before the creation of the world." (Ephesians 1:4 NIV) How could he choose us "in him" without first choosing *him*? The Godhead's decision to send Jesus was made in eternity with "prayer"… or with Divine communion.

That's why the Messianic Psalms discuss Jesus' incarnation before he was ever born. Psalm 2 portrays the Father saying "You are my son; today I have become your Father" and the 40th Psalm has the Messiah saying "a body you prepared for me" several hundred years before his own birth.

So as God's Son, Jesus' prayer life didn't begin on earth. He prayed - communed with the Father – even in eternity.

Prayer On Earth

Even after coming to earth, Jesus became the embodiment of intense prayer.

"During the days of Jesus' life on earth, he offered up prayers and petitions with loud cries and tears to the one who could save him from death, and he was heard because of his reverent submission." (Hebrews 5:7 NIV)

Even though he was sinless, Jesus stepped into the role of man estranged from God. When he prayed, the gap closed. He died, and was resurrected, praying all the time.

Prayer spanned the gulf between God and man. His whole death, burial and resurrection were bathed in prayer. Prayer, his prayers, healed the breach between God and man, shutting Satan out of the Garden of Eden for those who believe on Jesus' work.

To take on the role as substitute for sinful people, to live his life as a stand-in for us, and to atone for our sin by going to hell in our place... all of this demanded prayer. He couldn't be our representative, and be fully human, without bowing before his Father in prayer and submission.

So from his baptism to the cross, he prayed.

Prayer After The Cross

If you could peek into heaven right now, what would you see?

According to Revelation, you'd see the great throne of God surrounded by the four living creatures, the twenty four elders, the souls of the departed dead, angels without number and a splendor that can't be communicated in human language.

But you'd see something else; *you'd see a man praying.*

You'd see one of us, *Jesus*, who has been resurrected with a glorified human body equipped to move about the heavenly realm. He's one of a kind, at least until the resurrection day.

You'd see all that, and you'd see him *praying*: He's "able to save completely those who come to God through him, because he always lives to intercede for them." (Hebrews 7:25 NIV)

He's there as one of us. One of our specie has made it, and he hasn't forgotten us. He prays right now to restore the fallen human race back to God, destroying Satan's grip on us.

Jesus is so convinced that prayer is the key for restoring man to God that he refuses to stop even in heaven.

And he knows that if mankind (including him) abandons prayer, Satan wins. God *must* be continuously invited into the process, into the human situation. Jesus persists in it even now.

He *is* prayer. Without him, prayer wouldn't even be possible. He prayed before Adam drew a breath. He prayed in our skin while on this planet. He prays even now in heaven.

What do you suppose we could learn from *his* proactive prayer life?

The next few chapters will answer that question.

Chapter Two: HEAVEN WAS OPENED

"And as he was praying, heaven was opened and the Holy Spirit descended on him in bodily form like a dove. And a voice came from heaven: 'You are my son, whom I love; with you I am well pleased." (Luke 3:21-22 NIV)

Powerless?

It turned out to be a glorious day at the Tournament of Roses parade. New Year's Day. Chamber of Commerce weather. Magnificent floats passing by ... well, *all but one* passed by.

One of the most impressive floats sputtered and died right in front of the audience. The truck pulling it ran out of gas. That was amusing enough (the biggest parade of the year and someone forgot to fill the tank) but the crowd really roared when they realized whose truck ran out of gas ... The logo on the door said it belonged to Standard Oil, at the time one of the largest oil conglomerates in the nation! [1]

A company sitting on some of the world's largest oil reserves hadn't bothered to put enough gas in their truck to finish one parade.

Have you ever started a project and then ran out of the energy, money or time to finish it? We all have.

Have you ever started a project that died from neglect and apathy? So have I. Ever seen a group start an idealistic endeavor and then bury it in a quiet graveside service due to lack of interest? Sure you have. Me, too.

Have you ever seen a church drag along year after year with the fuel gauge hovering at "empty"? If so, it was probably a group of very sweet people who tried hard to follow Christ. They were sincere, yet the congregation never seemed to do more than keep the doors open. They had no dynamic power. No excitement. No unusual joy. No victories to speak of. No power to make a real difference in an insane world. No energy to turn the surrounding community upside down for Christ. No power to bring peace to a scared, stressed-out human race.

It's almost funny if it weren't so deadly serious. The Body of Christ sitting on *titanic* reserves of Divine energy, yet often too anemic to energetically administer life support to a world screaming for help.

Why? Why are we so weak in imitating Christ, especially when it comes to self-sacrificing service?

You'll find an answer when you look at this first photo in the picture album titled "The Prayer Habits of Jesus."

Starting Off With Power

It all started as John the Baptist positioned himself in the desert just north of the Dead Sea near a major north-south highway. Even in that remote spot, he drew massive crowds.

He drew them even though his messages weren't sweet sermonettes. He pounded away like heavy artillery at their hypocrisy. He thundered one theme: *repent!*

He demanded they get serious about honoring Jehovah through the Law by rejecting the pagan culture around them; he promised Divine wrath on those who wouldn't clean up their morals and prepare for Messiah.

As part of this repentance, John also demanded baptism. The Jews in John's day often practiced ritual washings, called the *mikveh*, to purify themselves and even to prepare for Yom Kippur, the Day of Atonement.

Yet while preaching his tough message of repentance and baptism, something happened that rattled the wilderness prophet. Jesus showed up to repent and be baptized!

Jesus, the only truly righteous Jew that John knew in all Israel, presents himself to John for ritual baptism just as any other backslidden Jew. An amazed John balks. He tries to deter Jesus: "I need to be baptized by you, and do you come to me?" (Matthew 3:14 NIV)

Jesus finally persuades him. The Sinless One enters Jordan's waters, immersed by John just like any perverted Jewish sinner who'd been unfaithful to Jehovah.

Amazing! Why did he submit to this demeaning ritual of repentance?

Because he's starting to fulfill his role as sin-bearer. God begins to lay on him "the iniquity of us all." (Isaiah 53:6 NIV) Shadows of the cross start forming at his feet. Now, after baptism, Jesus can begin his ministry ... but he doesn't, not yet.

First Things First

Instead of beginning his ministry right after his baptism, Jesus *prays*. But why pray now? Why does he postpone the mission and stop to consult his Father? Besides that, what's he asking for that's so important?

Let's take the simple approach. There must be some connection between what he prayed for and what he got. If you look at the answers he received, then you'll know his prayer's content.

"And as he was praying, heaven was opened and the Holy Spirit descended on him in bodily form like a dove. And a voice came from heaven: 'You are my Son, whom I love; with you I am well pleased.'" (Luke 3:21-22 NIV)

He asked for heaven to open, and it did. He asked for the Holy Spirit, and he came. He asked for the

Father's backing in this messianic mission, and God verbally responded. Through *prayer* Jesus received the supernatural stamp of approval and the power to carry out his awesome assignment.

Isn't that staggering? Here's the Only Begotten of the Father, full of grace and truth, and he needs prayer!

He needs prayer to withstand Satan's wilderness assault. He needs prayer to stay bonded to the Father's will. He needs prayer so he'll weather the storm of controversy coming at him. He needs prayer to lift him above the wrenching loneness of Gethsemane and the horrors of the cross.

The Son of God made his prayer life *proactive*, never just reacting to situations but bathing them in prayer in advance.

Why do believers today think we can get by without much prayer? Why do we think Jesus' followers today can operate in Divine energy without those golden hours spent in prayer? Why do we persist in ignoring Christ's example and his call for us to be a people of prayer?

Because sometimes our thinking isn't Biblical, at least in the area of prayer. A Scriptural mind-set demands we "devote ourselves to prayer" (Colossians 4:2 NIV) and "pray without ceasing." (1 Thessalonians 5:17 NIV) And that mind-set demands we follow Christ's lead.

If he prayed little, so can we, but if he prayed much, and with intense boldness, what about us? If prayer was his way of opening heaven, shouldn't it be ours also?

When prayer clears the path at the inception of a project, heaven opens and the effort is bathed in Divine energy. Then, a constant devotion to prayer keeps the tanks full of Divine energy.

Chapter Three: TOO BUSY TO PRAY

"Very early in the morning, while it was still dark, Jesus got up, left the house and went off to a solitary place, where he prayed." (Mark 1:35 NIV)

The Rat Race

Sometimes we call it the "Rat Race" - this high-tech, high-octane, high-volume life most of us endure today. We fantasize about escaping it. We know it's bad for us.

In fact, Dr. Joseph Buckley proved it. He used actual rats in real rat races to study just how much the Rat Race damages us. He subjected thousands of rats to a stress chamber designed to imitate modern life: jarring and jostling motions, flashing lights, noises ranging from buzzers to recorded jet aircraft sounds.

He found out it takes only a week. In only a week of this simulated Rat Race, the rats developed high blood pressure, becoming irritable and violent.

But the experiment had an unexpected side effect. According to Associated Press reports, the doctor and a graduate student *developed the same symptoms as the rats!* [2]

A Day In The Life

I wonder if Jesus ever felt like the demands of *his* schedule resembled rats racing. Sometimes we romanticize ancient times and assume those folks had leisurely lives: low-tech, low-stress, low-expectations. However, if you look closer you'll find the same potential for stress which we have. Sometimes a full schedule kept Jesus and his disciples from even having time to eat. (Mark 3:20)

Notice *this* schedule: It's one day in Jesus' life as recorded in Mark's Gospel, first chapter.

The day, a Sabbath, began in the Capernaum synagogue with a lengthy service: recitation of the Shema (confessions about Jehovah, taken from several Scriptures), the cycle of the Eighteen Prayers, readings from the Law with interpretation, readings from the Prophets with interpretation, a sermon (which Jesus delivered), collection for the poor, and benediction by a priest.

However, on this Sabbath the services probably ran longer. A demonized man cried out during Jesus' sermon, disrupting the service. Jesus cast the demon out and continued to teach.

Then after the synagogue service, Jesus and his disciples went to Peter's home. There they found Peter's mother-in-law sick with fever, so Jesus healed her.

The people who had been in the synagogue service buzzed with amazement about Jesus' authority, so the news about him spread that afternoon throughout the whole region. By sunset a crowd gathered at Peter's house, bringing all the sick and demonized people of the area. After dark the whole town of Capernaum gathered around the house to watch Jesus in action. Mark's account says he healed *many* and drove out *many* demons.

At some point in the late night hours, mercifully, Jesus' day ended. Was he weary? Even though he's God's Son, he still lived in a human body, a body with the same needs as ours for food, water, rest and relaxation.

But look at this. How did Jesus deal with this exhausting day? How did he recover? Did he crash on the couch till afternoon? Did he sleep-in the next day?

The Prayer Priority

"Very early in the morning, while it was still dark, Jesus got up, left the house and went off to a solitary place, where he prayed." (Mark 1:35 NIV)

Amazingly, he's up and praying "very early in the morning." Nothing could stagger Jesus' commitment to prayer. Too busy to pray? Never! He knew that if you're too busy to *pray*, you're just too busy.

Too tired to pray? No! His strength didn't come from constant rest, but constant prayer.

Spiritual apathy, the waste by-product of prayer-lessness, creeps up on you because of this simple mistake: *when the schedule gets crowded, prayer is the first thing left in the dust.* Let that happen and you lose perspective. Back to the Rat Race, running and circling but accomplishing little of real value.

When Peter and friends found Jesus at prayer that morning they said, "Everyone is looking for you!" They assumed Jesus would go back to the town and sun himself in the afterglow of yesterday's success.

Instead he said, "Let us go somewhere else - to the nearby villages - so I can preach there also." (Mark 1:38 NIV)

Notice how prayer had clarified his purpose. Instead of being trapped in a Capernaum Rat Race, he moved ahead in his ministry. He wasn't confused or indecisive about his next move. He didn't let a busy schedule kill his perspective or choke out his prayer life.

The Voice from the Prayer Closet

Prayer clarifies your purpose. It keeps you listening to the Voice and not just the voices around you. It gives you a perspective you can't get anywhere else.

Like the story of a football game in 1982 at Badger Stadium in Madison, Wisconsin as the University of Wisconsin team was being pounded mercilessly by rival Michigan State. The game grew worse and the score more lopsided, but several Wisconsin fans at the top of the stadium kept on cheering wildly, even though their team was losing.

Enduring dirty looks from the other Wisconsin fans, this enthusiastic entourage cheered even more. So, why were they ecstatic even though their team found itself on the embarrassing end of a lopsided score?

Well, they had a *different* perspective. Several miles away their other team, the Milwaukee Brewers, were winning game three of baseball's World Series. As they listened on their portable radios, they couldn't help but cheer. They connected to a source of joy unknown by those around them.

So it is with prayer. Connect yourself to the higher voice. Make time to pray; then watch joy, peace a better perspective return.

Chapter Four: JESUS' APPROACH TO MINISTRY

"Yet the news about him spread all the more, so that crowds of people came to hear him and to be healed of their sicknesses. But Jesus often withdrew to lonely places and prayed." **(Luke 5:15-16 NIV)**

Sharpening The Sword

Ever heard of an ichneumon? Strange little creature. It's small and looks a little like a weasel, but it can murder poisonous snakes a yard long. Even after being bitten repeatedly.

How? Well, it never attacks a snake unless it's near a certain plant whose leaves produce anti-venom sap. When bitten, the ichneumon rushes to the plant, nibbles the leaves, recovers and then attacks the snake again. [3]

Amazing. It's amazing how God arranged nature to teach spiritual laws. Like this law; it takes periods of withdrawal and renewal to win at spiritual warfare. Jesus knew that principle. He taught it. He lived it. He knew when to fight and when to sharpen his sword.

When the disciples found Jesus in the early-morning prayer session you saw in the last chapter, he said "Let us go somewhere else - to the nearby villages - so I can preach there also." (Mark 1:35 NIV) Luke now picks up the story in chapter five of his gospel:

Eye Of The Storm

This next preaching trip took Jesus to the working-class villages surrounding the Sea of Galilee. He taught at the water's edge then told his disciples to lower their nets. They reluctantly did, but all of a sudden the nets ripped apart and the boats swamped under the strain of a massive catch! What could they do but sit awe-struck and worship Jesus?

Then Jesus healed a leper; that caused a few jaws to drop. But the most electrifying part was when Jesus *touched* the leprous outcast. He actually put his hands on a man who was contagious and unclean under religious ceremonial law. Even though Jesus ordered the healed man to keep quiet, he couldn't.

So the news about Jesus spread like a fire in dry brush. All Galilee buzzed about him. Crowds mobbed him, anxious to hear him speak and watch him heal.

Into that frantic storm of popularity Luke injects this: "But Jesus often withdrew to lonely places and prayed." Jesus *often withdrew*. He withdrew to lonely places. He prayed. He bathed his entire Galilean ministry in prayer.

Often means with frequent regularity. Like *often* going fishing or *often* eating the same foods or *often* reading the Bible.

Jesus *often* made regular trips to unpopulated places to spend hours at a time praying. And he did it despite a hectic schedule full of awesome responsibilities.

To Jesus, withdrawal into prayer didn't mean he was ignoring the responsibilities of his ministry. No one born into this world ever had more responsibility placed on him than Jesus. Humanity's entire destiny literally balanced on his shoulders. He knew the awesome importance, the eternal weight, of his ministry: he came to seek and save the lost (Luke 19:10), to destroy Satan's power and free the human race (Hebrews 2:14), to draw all men to him (John 12:32), to give his life a ransom for many (Matthew 20:28).

These aren't lightweight goals. They aren't petty political agendas or foolishly idealistic social programs. They're the answer to humanity's deepest fears and needs. They strike at the heart of the cosmic warfare between good and evil, God and Satan.

And only one individual could accomplish them. So why did he take time away from the battle?

It's simple: *spiritual* combat requires *spiritual* energy. Prayer renews. It puts back the spiritual edge, sharpening the weapons of our warfare for the next battle.

Today's believers often stagger from Satan's venom, weakened in spiritual force and power. But prayer is the antidote. Reversing the poison's effect, prayer is God's creation for our survival against the snake's bite.

As his church, we're facing intense spiritual combat ahead. Can you tell the times are already dark? Haven't we already seen the "Brave New World," "Post-Christian Era," "New Age," and "Post-Modern World" emerging and challenging Christ for primacy in the mind-set market place? The neo-paganism flooding our world aims at one goal: to worship the creature rather than the Creator.

If that new emphasis on paganism wins, the church will face severe persecution soon (review the history of what always happens when paganism dominates a culture).

But if that rise in paganism is curbed, it'll be through a sweeping revival spurred by a cleansed, renewed and spiritually powerful church.

Are we ready for such spiritual combat? Not unless we're ready to pay the price. God's cause needs a generation of Christians with steel backbones, the mind of Christ, and calloused knees.

He needs those who'll often withdraw to lonely places and pray.

Chapter Five: THE DARK NIGHT OF DECISION

"One of those days Jesus went out to a mountainside to pray, and spent the night praying to God." **(Luke 6:12 NIV)**

Time To Listen

A Yellowstone Park Ranger herded his group of hikers toward the fire lookout tower. They almost didn't make it alive.

Along the trail, the Ranger got so caught up in telling about Yellowstone's unique wonders that he switched off the two-way radio on his belt; the squawking and crackling distracted from his lecture.

But as they came within sight of the fire tower, a breathless park employee ran toward the group: "*Grizzly bear!* We've been up in the tower, watching him stalk you ... we tried to call you on the radio ... what's wrong with your radio?!" [4]

The moral of the story? Things get dangerous when you stop listening, especially when you stop listening to God.

Have you ever done that? Ever gone off making decisions without listening, without asking God's advice, and then regretted it later? I have.

Have you ever set your course ("Here's my plan, God ... now please bless it") and then pulled your hair out trying to bail out a sinking project that didn't have Divine backing? You and I both know you have ... so have I.

What's wrong with that approach? It's pre-packaged disaster, that's all. That's why Jesus never conducted ministry that way. Notice how he kept contact with his Father, especially when fork-in-the-road decisions had to be made:

Why Pray So Long?

About the middle of Jesus' second ministry year, he started getting hateful opposition to his work. Because he claimed to forgive sins, and because he healed people on the Sabbath, his enemies decided to have him killed.

On top of that, he had another dilemma. Since his days on earth were numbered, someone would have to inherit his ministry. He would leave earth and leave his work behind ... in human hands!

The gospel would have to be preached by flawed, finite, corrupt people... people without much experience at *being Jesus*. Which ones should he choose? And how would they *ever* get enough training and spiritual knowledge to do a decent job of *replacing Christ!?*

Packing these two hot issues (First, how to handle Satan's plot to murder him and Second, whom should he choose to inherit this ministry) Jesus climbed the mountainside to pray.

"One of those days Jesus went out to a mountainside to pray, and spent the night praying to God." (Luke 6:12 NIV)

Be careful. We're standing on holy ground. We're witnessing something of the Divine mystery.

The Only Begotten Son of God. The Alpha and Omega. The Holy One of Israel. The Lion of Judah. The Prince of Peace. The Word, who was with God and *was God. He* is *praying*. He *asks for his Father's help.* They converse all night long.

The next morning Jesus chose the Twelve.

Do you realize that the leadership plan of the church itself emerged that night in prayer? Before he began to transfer any authority to his followers, Jesus spent the whole night praying. It all began with prayer.

Why? Did the Son of God *need* to pray? If not, what he did was a sham, an empty exercise in deception. If he didn't truly pray and his Father didn't truly listen and answer, then the Bible is a lie.

Yes, Jesus *needed* prayer. He needed it because of his kinship with us as a human being. Do we need prayer any less? The Father's ordained way of working with human issues on this planet is by *prayer*.

Whatever the project and however small its beginning, it needs prayer first. I'm trying to learn to pray more at the beginning of things, rather than later after the wheels have come off. Why not just pray for the church (as Jesus did) rather than wrangling over church politics, programs, or the latest gimmicks to inspire church growth.

Is it because we pray so little that we have such meager results ... and such shallow leadership?

Did It Work?

Even though the men Jesus appointed as apostles weren't perfect, as a whole they (through the Holy Spirit) got the job done. They didn't quit. Eleven of them weathered physical abuse and some were even martyred, yet they remained true to Jesus' mission.

Jesus' prayer *worked*. His night on the mountain is still here; it looms as one of his greatest time-investments.

And the early church learned from his mentoring:

The leaders at Antioch sent Paul and Barnabus into the mission field this way: "So after they had fasted and prayed they placed their hands on them and sent them off." (Acts 13:3 NIV)

This wasn't a quick Sunday morning send-off (you can't fast in twenty minutes.) It took hours ... days. The Antioch leaders *spent days fasting and praying to get these two men ready for upcoming spiritual combat.*

And even as Paul and Barnabus did the work, they applied the same principle: "Paul and Barnabus appointed elders for them in each church and, with prayer and fasting, committed them to the Lord, in whom they had put their trust." (Acts 14:23 NIV)

From Jesus, to the Antioch leaders, to Paul and Barnabus - the cycle continued. And for us also, the cycle *must* continue. Bathe every decision in prayer. Spend hours in prayer and fasting to make sure God's plan is first, not ours.

Tune in to God. After all, something might be stalking you.

Chapter Six: WALKING ON PRAYER

"After he had dismissed them, he went up a mountainside by himself to pray." (Matthew 14:23 NIV)

Stormy Weather

H.G. Bosch couldn't believe it. How could a 400 foot tall iceberg keep bulling its way south right into the teeth of a stiff head wind? Against thundering surf?

The answer (warning: here comes a parable) lies beneath the surface; 90% of an iceberg's mass is below the water line. According to a ship's officer that Bosch queried, the icebergs he saw were in the Labrador Current – a massive ocean highway headed relentlessly south. As the current goes, so goes the iceberg. [5]

Isn't life just like that? (I told you there was a parable.) On the surface, some people seem so in control of themselves. They seem to have life all figured out ... until tragedy arrives. Until the storm builds and life kicks them in the teeth.

Then they're revealed for what they really were all along. Dead inside, like Jesus' reference to the Pharisees, "whitewashed tombs"... sparkling outside, foul inside.

But others keep cruising into stiff head winds and crushing surf. Their values are a constant, refusing to change with the weather. They have character. They relentlessly track toward God, no matter how loudly the dogs of contemporary culture bark.

Jesus was such a man. He knew that anyone who marries the spirit of his times will soon be a widower. He knew he had to do his Father's will even if it hurt, even if it killed him. Where did he find such courage? Watch as it unfolds.

Notice how Matthew describes this next major event in Jesus' prayer life:

Jesus had just started the last year of his earthly work. The religious professionals stirred a passionate opposition to him, and it was growing more hateful.

John the Baptist, Jesus' cousin, was beheaded. His death sent aftershocks through Jesus' camp. How would the Master deal with it?

He got into a boat and headed for a *solitary place* so he could pray (Matthew 14:13). But he couldn't avoid the crowds. They followed him from all over Galilee, swarming by the thousands to intercept him as he landed on the other shore.

When he saw them he couldn't refuse. Compassion impelled him to heal the sick. He even spent the whole day with them. By evening they needed food, so he took five loaves and two fish and fed all 5,000 people.

But then the situation grew more intense; the crowd wanted to take Jesus to Jerusalem and make him Jewish king by force of arms (John 6:15). After all, who'd make a better king? Who wouldn't want a king who could raise fallen warriors back to life and feed whole armies with one ration? Why not attack the Romans in Jerusalem and make Jesus king by force?

With the tension at a snapping point, Jesus ordered his disciples into the boat and sent them back across the Sea of Galilee. He dismissed the crowds before anything could come of their heady plan.

Finally, after a whole day's interruptions, Jesus headed for a quiet place to pray.

All Night In Prayer

He had much to pray about: John the Baptist's death at Herod's whim, his own impending cross, the danger that crowds of people would start a revolutionary blood bath in his name, the inexperience of his disciples. These dilemmas, and the interruptions of the day, impelled Jesus into *another* all-night prayer session.

According to Matthew, "When evening came, he was there alone" (14:23 NIV). By the fourth watch of the night, Jesus had finished praying and headed back across the Sea of Galilee.

Evening meant the time right after supper, and the fourth watch is 3:00 to 6:00 A.M. - so Jesus had prayed about eight hours that night.

This may seem odd to some people. Why spend so much time in prayer when there's important work to get done? At least, why not rest up for tomorrow's work? Why stress yourself out by *staying up all night and praying?* For some, it's hard to understand Jesus' priority on prayer.

As J.W. McGarvey a preacher in early America commented about Jesus' prayer: "Why he spent so long a time in prayer, it is difficult for us who know so little of the value of prayer, and so little of the inner life of Jesus, to understand." [6]

The key to understanding this remarkable prayer life is this: look at the *result* of his praying.

Walking On Prayer

While Jesus prayed for eight hours, the disciples had rowed. They made little progress; persistent head winds and swelling waves kept them from crossing the lake in that eight hours.

Stiff from an all-night struggle against this restless sea, the disciples sat amazed when they saw Jesus walking on the same swells. *He strolled along on the power of his own prayers.*

Against the wind, against the surf, against the normal laws of nature, Jesus calmly, confidently walked. While the water alone couldn't support his weight, his all night praying buoyed him up on a liquid sidewalk. His walking on water wasn't a magician's stunt, but proof that *prayer can do anything God can do.*

At first, the disciples thought he was a ghost. They screamed in fear, but he calmed them by calling out. When Peter recognized his voice, he asked permission to try the same thing ... walking on the sea! (He instinctively knew that disciples should imitate their Rabbi.)

Amazingly, Peter looked like Jesus for a short while as he made his way toward the Teacher on the violent sea, but soon his faith ran out of fuel. Remember, *Jesus had prayed all night* but Peter knew little of this Divine wellspring of supernatural power. He walked on the strength of Jesus' command, but he didn't have the spiritual iceberg of a whole night in prayer under him as Jesus did. He found it difficult to imitate the Master's walking for long without tasting of Jesus' brand of praying beforehand.

See the contrast? The man of prayer boldly walks, carried along on the storm by the intense energy of his prayers, while the occasional dabbler in prayer sinks in surrender to the choking circumstances around him.

When Jesus stepped into the boat, all was calm. The sea calmed and their fears calmed, because the man who had prayed all night brought the fruit of his prayers into their struggle. He had prayed alone on the mountain, and then brought his friends a special harvest - peace in the middle of chaos.

Like the iceberg charging into the face of stiff winds and waves, Jesus' power lay below the surface ... in his prayer life.

The same is true now. If we plan to calm frantic souls brutalized by a Satanic spiritual storm, we *must* pray. We must develop another *great awakening of prayer* in the church, moving us ahead by powers below the surface.

You can touch the invisible and sail like an iceberg against the tides of a sinking culture, but only *if* you first tap the powers below the surface.

Chapter Seven: PRAYER & HARD TEACHINGS

"Once when Jesus was praying in private and his disciples were with him, he asked them, 'who do the crowds say I am?'" **(Luke 9:18 NIV)**

Vision Problems

When Henry J. Ellsworth resigned as Commissioner of the U.S. Patent Office, he said he wouldn't be missed. "Mankind has already achieved all of which it is capable. There would be no more inventions requiring patents." [7]

He said that in 1844. Before the steamboat, electric lights, telephones, automobiles, aircraft, computers and space flight.

Ellsworth was wrong, but he wasn't alone. When a U.S. Congressman rose to speak about balancing the federal budget, he listed the staggering number of entries at the Patent Office and then concluded that Congress should close it.

Why? Because, he said, nothing else could possibly be invented. He made that speech in the early 1870's. [8]

Why does that creative vision escape us so often? Too many of us are like the Hollywood talent judge watching a screen test in 1932 who wrote the following about an eager young performer: "Can't act. Can't sing. Can dance a little."

The guy who could dance "a little" was Fred Astaire. [9]

Need more evidence that we sometimes lack vision? One football expert evaluated a young coach this way: "He possesses minimal football knowledge. Lacks motivation." The young coach? Vince Lombardi. [10]

Obviously it's hard to find open minds, especially about human potential. That's why one newspaper editor fired Walt Disney from a job; he said Disney didn't have any good ideas. [11]

Well, it's one thing to misjudge a talented person. But it's quite another to misunderstand God's timing and movements. And to misjudge God's Messiah.

Warning: Hard Sayings

How did Jesus deal with this human problem of low vision, of having a tendency to misevaluate the genius? How did Jesus prevent sincere people from stumbling over him?

You're probably guessing that prayer had something to do with it. It did. Just before Jesus polled his disciples about human opinions of his work, he *prayed.*

If you combine the four gospel accounts of the incident, you get the following scenario:

After Jesus fed the 5,000, he prayed all night. He then walked to his disciples on the Sea of Galilee during the 4th watch - 3:00 to 6:00 A.M.

As the crowds tracked him down the next day because he'd fed them, he accused them of only looking for more food, and then taught some startling information. *He* is the bread they should seek out. Men must eat his flesh and drink his blood to have eternal life!

Hearing this, a group of his disciples complained "This is a hard teaching. Who can accept it?" (John 6:60 NIV) From that day forward, crowds of disciples turned back and no longer followed him (John 6:66).

According to Luke's account, Jesus then turned to prayer. He knew that more hard teachings were on the way. Could his disciples take it? Would they understand? Would it drive them away?

After praying, he asked, "Who do the crowds say I am?" (Luke 9:18 NIV) They answered by telling him what they'd heard, that many compared him to the great prophets such as John the Baptist or Elijah.

Then he popped the question: "Who do you say I am?" Peter said, "You are the Christ, the Son of the living God."

Notice Jesus' response to Peter's answer: "Blessed are you ... this was not revealed to you by man, but by my Father in heaven." (Matthew 16:17 NIV) Only *God* had softened Peter's heart and protected his understanding ... *in answer to Jesus' prayers*.

With that foundation laid, Jesus embarked on even more hard teaching: that he must suffer, be rejected by the Jewish leaders, be put to death and be raised on the third day.

Peter became so agitated that he took Jesus aside and privately rebuked him for such depressing ideas. Jesus reaction? "Get behind me, Satan!" (Matthew 16:23 NIV)

Then came *more* tough teachings. Not only was Messiah going to the cross, but anyone who followed him would die, too. "If anyone would come after me, he must deny himself and take up his cross and follow me." (Matthew 16:24 NIV)

The lessons weren't getting any easier. And the disciples weren't getting any happier. Things got uncomfortable. Souls hung in the balance. That's why Jesus prayed... so his disciples' hearts would stay soft, open to these demanding teachings.

But *how do we know* that's what he prayed for? Well, context is everything. No one prays in a vacuum, especially not Jesus. His prayers dealt with the concerns that swirled around him right then. His disciples' hearts needed protection, so his prayers took up that issue.

Remote Heart Surgery?

Does prayer *really* influence other people? Can prayer protect their attitudes while they evaluate hard teachings? Can it energize their spiritual vision? Does prayer change human minds?

Did you know that every letter the Apostle Paul wrote to the churches (except Galatians) starts with a section about prayer?

Did you know that Ephesians, Philippians and Colossians begin with major sections about Paul's prayers for the *hearts*, the spiritual growth of his readers?

Just like Jesus, Paul and the other apostles used prayer to influence hearts.

Did you know that the ancient church considered prayer just as important a tool as preaching for changing hearts; that when the apostles decided to give their "attention to prayer and the ministry of the word" the church grew like a wildfire, even among Jewish *priests*? (Acts 6:4-7 NIV)

And it still happens that way; even whole nations can be changed by prayer. In fact, Andrew Murray once said that the "whole religious tone of Scotland has been lifted up" after the visit of one preacher to the British Isles, Dwight L. Moody.

But Moody, a famous evangelist of the nineteenth century, didn't even intend to preach while in Britain. He came to rest and to hear other great preachers such as Charles Spurgeon and George Muller.

Yet he reluctantly gave in when a local preacher in London prevailed on him to preach one Sunday in his church. Mr. Moody preached on that Sunday morning, but found it hard work. The lifeless congregation vacantly gazed at him while he tried to preach, so he politely put the doomed sermon out of its misery as quickly as he could. And what was worse, he had promised to preach again that night!

But while preaching that night, Moody noticed a different spirit in the same group. And when he ended his sermon by asking if any wished to become Jesus' disciples, the people stood in large groups. Moody was unsure that they heard correctly, so he restated his case and even more stood! He even asked them to reconvene in a nearby room to make sure they all understood, and the room soon filled up with eager faces and willing hearts.

So, what had happened to make such a change in one afternoon? A bedridden woman named Marianne Adlard had prayed. In fact, she had prayed for Mr. Moody to come to her church while he was still thousands of miles away in America.

And when her sister came home from the morning service to tell Marianne that a man from America named Moody had preached, she sat up in bed, refused her lunch and began praying for Moody's success at the evening service.

D.L. Moody continued his trip by traveling to Dublin, but he was recalled to that London church the next day because more people had come on Monday to hear about salvation. He preached there for the next ten days; four hundred people came to Christ and revival began to sweep the British Isles,

all because of an unknown woman's intense praying.
[12]

Even today believers who take prayer seriously, who pray tirelessly for hearts inside and outside God's kingdom, these will make the greatest progress in changing the attitudes of others.

If we aren't praying, we're missing out. We're overlooking the *greatest power God ever created to change human hearts.*

Besides, only God can change a heart. The God who hardened Pharaoh's and opened Lydia's is the same God who'll melt hearts today ... if we *pray.*

Chapter Eight: PRAYER & TRANSFORMATION

"As he was praying the appearance of his face changed, and his clothes became as bright as a flash of lightning." (Luke 9:29 NIV)

Faces Of Prayer

She called late one afternoon. I could tell she was crying.

"My husband and I had a big fight... Please come; I've got to talk to someone!"

I didn't know her very well. I had just moved to the church as their new preacher, besides, she and her husband didn't attend much. Despite that, since she was desperate, my wife and I went.

I'll admit I was nervous. Nervous about walking into a marital minefield. Yelling. Screaming. A torrent of negative energy.

That's why I was so relieved when we arrived *after the husband had left*. (He had stormed out and gone to a buddy's house to cool off.)

So we sat with this distraught woman at the kitchen table while she unloaded all her marital grief. I sat a little bewildered not having much experience at marriage counseling, yet we listened.

But then *he* unexpectedly came back home... came home to find strangers in his house, to find the new preacher listening to intimate details about his troubled marriage. I could see the combination of anger, shock and irritation in his face.

He sat down with us, but was uneasy. It wasn't a comfortable conversation and the small talk just wasn't working; I could tell he was getting more irritated. At that point, I decided we should cut our losses and leave.

"Would it be all right if we have a prayer?" I asked.

Before anyone had time to object, I bowed and began praying. I prayed for each of them, for their marriage, their children, their spiritual lives and for the church in general. After about five minutes, I ended the prayer and looked up ... and sat amazed.

All the anger had drained from his face. It reminded me of times when we had nursed our children through fevers and watched the danger suddenly pass as a twinkle returned to the eyes.

I'd seen remarkable answers to prayer before, but I still sat awed by how quickly prayer changed this man's attitude and the emotional landscape of his home. He relaxed so much that we stayed and had a productive counseling session and eventually became good friends.

One fantastic by-product of prayer is its ability to transform personality. When you draw near to God, he draws near to you; that creates transformation. You can't help being drawn in and changed by intimacy with God, anymore than iron filings can resist a magnet.

Why does prayer so radically transform human personality? Because it opens heaven. It brings a heavenly consciousness to earth. Heaven can invade earth during a powerful prayer experience. Ask Jesus. It happened to him. Here's how:

At Heaven's Gate

After giving the disciples about a week to digest his hard teachings, Jesus took Peter, James and John up the mountain to pray. To *pray*. His purpose in taking them up there was to pray and to have them witness the kind of praying that could open heaven's gate.

According to Luke's account, they didn't come down till the next day. They spent all night and part of two days on that mountain... praying.

Remember the context. It's well into Jesus' last year on earth. His enemies are gearing up for his trial. Whole crowds of disciples have quit in anger because of his teachings. The cross continues to stalk him.

While on the mountain, Jesus wraps himself up in his Father's embrace and holds on. He prays hour after hour. His intensity surpasses (by miles) our polite, sanitized Sunday morning praying.

While his disciples sleep, he gazes into his heavenly homeland's power and glory; it'll steel him for the horrors ahead.

Jesus prays so masterfully that he steps into the interface between heaven and earth. The boundary fades. He prays at the membrane between the Divine dimension and earthly life and finds himself transformed:

"As he was praying, the appearance of his face changed, and his clothes became as bright as a flash of lightning. Two men, Moses and Elijah, appeared in glorious splendor, talking with Jesus. They spoke about his departure, which he was about to bring to fulfillment at Jerusalem." (Luke 9:29-30 NIV)

Heaven opened and the two worlds, for a few moments, merged. Jesus' Divine spirit vibrated so intensely to heaven's glory that its light overtook his body. Moses and Elijah crossed the membrane for a conference on the crucifixion.

Keep this in mind. All this happened *in prayer*. It didn't happen as he walked along the road, or as he sat in the synagogue, or as he healed the sick, or as he taught the crowds ... it happened in *prayer*.

While we won't be *transfigured* in prayer (at least until the resurrection), we will be *transformed*. Put yourself under the search light of prayer and watch God reshape you.

Like wax melting in the sun, prayer puts you in Jesus' warming presence. As a caterpillar transforms from a worm to a soaring work of art, prayer splits the cocoon and releases your transformed spiritual personality.

Andrew Murray put it this way: "Prayer is, above all, fellowship with God and being brought under the power of holiness ... until He ... stamps our entire nature with the lowliness of Christ."[13]

Chapter Nine: A HABIT OF PRAISE

"At that time Jesus, full of joy through the Holy Spirit, said, 'I praise you Father, Lord of heaven and earth..." **(Luke 10:21 NIV)**

Prayer's Voice

W.E. Sangster, a British minister of the early 20th Century, went to his doctor and complained of numbness in his leg and throat. He got bad news; the doctor found an incurable muscle disease that would soon kill the preacher.

After his voice had deteriorated, he wrote his daughter a letter on Easter Sunday just two weeks before he died: "It is terrible to wake up on Easter morning and have no voice to shout, 'He is risen!' - but it would be still more terrible to have a voice and not want to shout." [14] Standing in the shallows of death's tide tends to clear one's thinking. That's why

Sangster's letter cuts through to the truth... Even when things are tough, it's better to praise God than to live in a Death Valley of arid unbelief.

So while your prayers have the voice of praise, use it! Jesus did. He mastered the art of weaving praise into his prayers. For him, it was natural. Notice how he did so in the following story.

Jesus' Reaction to Answered Prayer

Jesus appointed seventy-two disciples to go ahead of him in pairs into the villages he was about to visit. He gave them special instructions: (1) Pray for the Lord of the harvest to send workers, (2) Go as lambs among wolves, (3) Take no money but rely on the hospitality of villagers, (4) Heal the sick, and (5) Preach that the Kingdom of God is near.

With these orders, he crafted a direct frontal assault, a bold plan to gain a beachhead in Satan's kingdom, an attack designed to displace the kingdom of darkness by overpowering it with the Kingdom of God. His strategy launched an unvarnished challenge to Satan's lordship. And it worked.

It worked so well that the disciples came back cheering. "Lord, even the demons submit to us in your name." (Luke 10:17 NIV)

Jesus replied, "I saw Satan fall like lightning from heaven." (10:18 NIV)

With this victory, Jesus burst into praise: "At that time Jesus, full of joy through the Holy Spirit, said, 'I praise you, Father, Lord of heaven and earth, because you have hidden these things from the wise

and learned, and revealed them to little children.'"
(10:21 NIV)

His Father's victorious use of ordinary people
made Jesus "full of joy through the Holy Spirit." The
original Greek manuscripts of this verse use a word
that means "to leap for joy."And that overwhelming
joy caused Jesus to say, "I praise you…" which is to
say, "I agree totally that you have done this remarkable thing."

Isn't that the heartbeat of prayer? Isn't prayer
based on the fundamental idea that God hears, that
God cares and God answers? That's what Jesus
recognized, and what he used as a foundation for
this spontaneous prayer of praise. When Satan fell in
defeat, praise wasn't far behind.

Notice the connection. With the Father's consent,
Jesus had chosen seventy-two ordinary people (not
even part of the Twelve). He sent these ordinary folks
out with his own authority, which they used to heal
the sick and scatter demons. Satan's kingdom shut-
tered violently under the weight of Jesus' authority
exercised by everyday people; this awesome victory
in the cosmic war between God and Satan came at
the hands of *seventy-two ordinary people!*

And which humans did he use? Not the intel-
lectuals. Not the elite. Not the rich or the politically
connected. Not even the religious leaders. He used
ordinary people, people whose only credentials came
from Jesus.

The whole episode was undeniably a "God
thing." And for the devil, it was the end's beginning.
No wonder Jesus praised his Father!

Faith Speaks

And notice how this praise emerged. As naturally as one draws a breath, Jesus stopped in the middle of a conversation to address his Father. He wasn't timid about praising God out loud. He gave his Father immediate credit for the victory that just happened.

Faith speaks up. It speaks when it sees God's hand behind the scenes. Doubt clams up because it never sees God's hand in anything.

So a mature prayer life isn't possible without this element of wonder, of praise, of being awe-struck by God showing up inside time and space. Even the Lord's Model Prayer begins with this element: "Hallowed be your name."

In fact, most of the Bible's great prayers have the same aroma. Moses wrote a song of praise after seeing Jehovah part the Red Sea (Exodus 15). He worshipped again after hearing God's seminar on holiness (Exodus 34:8).

Hannah praised God for giving her a son named Samuel (which means, "heard by God"), even though she was barren (1 Samuel 2). Solomon dedicated his lavish temple with overflowing praise (2 Chronicles 6-7). King Jehoshaphat and his people praised Jehovah for victory before it even happened (2 Chronicles 20).

Nehemiah's prayer for Jerusalem's rebuilding begins first with praise (Nehemiah 1:5).

Prayers in the Psalms overflow with worship and praise. Proverbs promises that the path to wisdom begins with praise - the fear of Jehovah. Ecclesiastes warns the reader to stand in awe of God (Chapter 5).

Even the prophets, from Isaiah to Malachi, brim with praise and worship for Jehovah's mighty actions.

And as the New Testament opens, praises erupt for Christ's birth (Luke 2), for God's working within the church (Acts 2:47 & 4:23-31), for the Father's brilliant plan (Romans 11:33), and for God's victory over Satan through the church in Revelation.

Even today, a mature prayer life includes this element of praise, of understanding that answered prayers aren't just coincidence or good luck.

Praise gives God credit when he works, without doubting that he answered the prayer. Jesus *agreed* in his prayer that the Father had invaded Satan's kingdom, that no one else could take credit for it.

How Faith Prays

And that aroma of praise should fill every prayer, even *before* it is answered.

John Bisagno told of a woman who asked him to pray for her husband to be saved. He asked her if she had been praying for her own husband's salvation, and she replied that she had... for thirty five years!

Curious as to why she had seen no answers yet, Bisagno asked if she were praying like this: "Lord, if it by thy will save my husband"? She admitted that her prayers sounded just like that.

He then agreed to help her pray for her husband on one condition, that she stop praying that way and begin to *thank God that he was going to save her husband.* He then showed her places in the Bible where God states that he doesn't want any man to perish, but that he wants all to come to Christ (1 Timothy 2:4).

Bisagno intended for this woman to pray in faith based on Scripture. In other words, she was to *praise God beforehand* for the promised answer.

The next night when this woman came to church to hear Bisagno preach, her husband was with her; he committed his life to Christ that same night.

In his book on prayer Bisagno says, "One hour of praying in faith, believing, had done more good than thirty five years of endless repetition and doubting hesitation!" [15]

So how can your prayer life be considered complete without this element of praise? How can we invade the satanic kingdom and win souls without standing in awe of God?

As Paul Billheimer once wrote, "Satan is allergic to praise, so where there is massive triumphant praise, Satan is paralyzed, bound, and banished." [16]

Chapter Ten: PAYING THE PRICE

"One day Jesus was praying in a certain place. When he finished, one of his disciples said to him, 'Lord, teach us to pray, just as John taught his disciples.'" (Luke 11:1 NIV)

Serious About Prayer

Some people have paid remarkable prices just to pray.

Charles Simeon often spent four hours, from 4:00 to 8:00 A.M., in prayer.

Joseph Alleine would arise at 4:00 A.M. to pray until 8:00; he'd feel ashamed if he heard tradesmen doing business in the streets before he was at his prayers.

Robert Murray McCheyne prayed from 6:00 to 8:00 A.M., but also prayed any time he woke up in the night, and prayed again after breakfast.

Sir Henry Havelock also spent the first two hours of every day praying. No matter how early his day began, he'd arise two hours early to pray.

Adoniram Judson prayed two to three hours per day. He often recommended the same plan to others, as well as the idea of praying seven times per day.

The Marquis DeRenty once ordered his servant to call him after his prayer time, usually half of an hour. When he went to call the Marquis, he couldn't. DeRenty's face beamed with such intensity that the servant didn't dare interrupt. He finally got up the courage to interrupt the Marquis... *after three and a half hours.* When interrupted, the nobleman remarked how short thirty minutes seemed while communing with the Lord!

John Fletcher prayed so much that his warm breath stained the wallpaper of his room as he knelt against it. He sometimes prayed all night long.

John Welch of Scotland thought his day wasted unless he spent eight to ten hours in prayer. His wife would often find him up at night wrapped in a plaid blanket and praying. [17]

When I mention these people in prayer seminars, I get mixed reactions.

Some sit amazed; they can't believe people would pray like that. Some wonder what was wrong with these people: Did they have a problem? Didn't they understand God's love?

Some are put off by it, thinking these people must've been warped religious fanatics. Some think it smells of legalism, like earning one's way to heaven by long prayers.

Hungry For Prayer

But some get convicted by it. It touches them. They feel a kinship with these praying people. They want to pray like that; at least, they want to reach for a higher plane in prayer.

That must be how that disciple felt. You know, the one who heard Jesus praying. He asked, "Lord, teach us to pray, just as John taught his disciples."

Notice what he actually asked. He didn't ask, "Teach us *how* to pray." And he didn't ask, "Teach us *what* to pray." He asked, "Teach us *to* pray." In other words, "Lord, motivate us to pray… teach us to pray as you do… help us grasp the power of discipline and commitment in prayer…teach us to put prayer at the top of our priority list."

It's true that Jesus then gave them advice about the content of prayer, *what* to pray for (Luke 11:1-13). But he followed that with nine verses encouraging them *to* pray. He reassured them that the Father will answer the persistent seeker.

So, what made this disciple ask, "Lord, teach us *to* pray"?

Well, he asked partly because of John the Baptist's influence, who had taught his disciples *to* pray. John's ministry promoted moral purity and spiritual revival in Israel so the nation would be ready for Messiah.

Therefore, John's ministry included a *major emphasis on prayer*. His work must've included a massive, organized effort to motivate prayer among his disciples. That's because spiritual revival and prayer are twins. Where you find one, you find the other.

(Did you notice that the two greatest world-changers in history, Jesus and John the Baptist, regularly taught their disciples *to pray*?)

Jesus Paid The Price

But the disciple's request came for another reason. He'd seen Jesus pray. Jesus' prayer life itself had sparked a hunger for more. He wanted more out of prayer ... more weight, more intensity, more intimacy.

These disciples had watched Jesus' prayer life at close range for about two years. They knew he had faced Satan and defeated him because of forty days of prayer and fasting. They saw him cleanse the temple because he was angered that his Father's house of prayer had become a den of robbers.

They'd seen him heal thousands, win over whole villages, cast out demonic powers, feed thousands with one meal, experience transfiguration, walk on water, calm storms and teach as one with authority, all because of his *prayer life*.

And they *knew he prayed constantly*. He prayed all night before choosing the Twelve (Luke 6:12), before walking on the sea (Matthew 14:23-25) and during the transfiguration (Luke 9:28-37).

Later they discovered that Jesus considered a one hour prayer a short one when he asked, "Could you men not keep watch with me for one hour?" (Matthew 26:40 NIV)

God's own Son believed prayer to be an *indispensable link* with his Father in heaven; he prayed often, for long periods of time, and he prayed loyally. His prayers rocked the whole universe.

So his disciples hungered to know this kind of prayer first hand. They must've been convinced of one thing: *His power on earth came from his power in prayer*. And his power in prayer came from hours of praying.

He was their Rabbi, their mentor, their Master. They hungered to emulate him in all things, especially in prayer.

And so it is today, at least with many of his modern disciples. Do we want *his* kind of prayer life, even if it takes hours per day to secure it? Are we willing to pay the price he paid to pray as he prayed?

E.M. Bounds once wrote, "God's acquaintance is not made hurriedly. He does not bestow his gifts on the casual or hasty comer and goer. To be much alone with God is the secret of knowing Him and of influence with Him." [18]

Chapter Eleven: INVADING THE INVISIBLE

"So they took away the stone. Then Jesus looked up and said, 'Father, I thank you that you have heard me.'" (**John 11:41 NIV**)

Preparing For Battle

It happens every fall in Alaska. The bullmoose gather for mating season, which means the males battle each other for dominance. They always go head first, sometimes even shattering their antlers.

According to National Geographic, those same bulls feed all summer long in preparation for the fall contest. Moose that find the best diet for gaining weight and growing massive antlers always win the dominance war in the fall. Like most contests, the battle is decided in the *preparation stage* long before the warriors hit the battlefield. [19]

Jesus knew that principle, lived it, and projected himself as an example of it, especially in prayer. He never left the battle to chance. He knew that any spiritual warfare is won in the prayer closet before it's won on the field.

Can you think of any greater contest than facing down *death*? Is there anything more tenacious than death? Once it gets its icy grip on a person, it separates spirit from body and the victim lies beyond human help. What was once a person becomes a thing. There's nothing more final than a funeral.

But when Jesus approached Lazarus' tomb, death cowered in the corner. It was about to meet its match.

Notice how Jesus readied himself to snatch Lazarus back from the beyond.

After they removed the stone that spanned the mouth of Lazarus' tomb, Jesus looked up to heaven and said, "Father, I thank you that you have heard me."

He didn't say, "Father, I thank you that you *are hearing* me." He said "*heard*" ... that's past tense. He's talking about previous prayers, which he prayed long before he stood at the tomb. And he's *praying in faith by speaking of the answer in past tense.*

That shouldn't surprise us; prayers of faith often preceded major events in Jesus' ministry. He prayed all night before choosing the Twelve (Luke 6:12). He prayed all night before walking on the Sea of Galilee (Matthew 14:23-25). His transfiguration came during a night spent on the mountain in prayer (Luke 9:28-29). He bathed his whole life and ministry in prayer.

Even before he came to earth he "prayed"; he and the Father discussed his future physical birth (Hebrews 10:5).

And while on earth "he offered up prayers and petitions with loud cries and tears to the one who could save him from death, and he was heard because of his reverent submission." (Hebrews 5:7 NIV) *Even Jesus' own resurrection was an answer to prayer!*

Even after leaving earth he still prays, interceding for us right now as our supernatural high priest (Hebrews 7:25).

So throughout his ministry, prayer remained Jesus' natural home ground. When he prayed here on earth, he merely continued the eternal conversation that had forever flowed between Jesus and his Father.

For him, prayer opened heaven and extended the throne room life right here to earth. Prayer was central to his mission. It kept him in perfect unison with the Father's will. It gave him heaven's powers ... even over death.

Prayer Raises The Dead

Standing at Lazarus' tomb, Jesus gave credit aloud to prayer's power to raise the dead. He wanted his Father to have the praise for this remarkable rescue.

Jesus' power to raise Lazarus *came through prayer*. Even though he was, and is, the Son of God, he still was human. His body and human personality needed the Father's help to maintain power. He didn't work miracles with magic wands or strange incantations, but by power from heaven. Therefore, he needed prayer to maintain the fellowship ... and the power.

Does that sound odd? Would it surprise you to know that Jesus' power over Satanic evil varied at times?

Once when a sick woman touched his clothing, Jesus felt the power leave his body (Luke 8:46). One day when he was teaching, "the power of the Lord was present for him to heal the sick" (Luke 5:17 NIV). Even in his own home town "he did not do many miracles there because of their lack of faith." (Matthew 13:58 NIV) All of this tells me that his power must've varied daily.

Remember this. Even though he was God's Son here on earth, his pre-resurrection body wasn't indestructible. It was like ours. His body needed sleep, food and water, and his spirit needed time alone with the Father.

Therefore, *prayer helped him fulfill his mission* because it gave him power over the devil's work, allowing him to "bind the strong man" (Matthew 12:29).

So Jesus stood at Lazarus' tomb fully prepared. He had prayed. He had fed on his Father's glory until he stood there vibrating with spiritual energy, ready to invade the regions of the dead and wrench the keys of death and Hades from Satan's cold fist.

His faith drank so deeply of his Father's power that he came prepared to invade the strong man's house and assault "him who holds the power of death - that is, the devil" (Hebrews 2:14 NIV).

Jesus arrived to deliver the first eviction notice to that "last enemy to be destroyed ... death" (1 Corinthians 15:26 NIV).

"Lazarus, come out!"

And Lazarus came out. It's one of the greatest tributes to the power of prayer we'll ever see. Through prayer, Jesus had invaded the invisible and rescued a helpless man from death's choking stench.

Seeing Jesus' tenacious prayer life result in tomb-splitting power… shouldn't that motivate us? Since we've been given the mission of snatching a lost population from Satan's death grip, shouldn't we imitate our Mentor's prayer life so we can have a serving of his power? Since we know it's the key to power, shouldn't we make a pact with him to emulate his prayer habits?

That's the only way we'll ever storm the gates of hell, shake it to its foundations and rescue the zombie-like men and women who shuffle around this earth in a death-walk, staggering under Satan's oppression.

E.M. Bounds said it this way: "What the church needs today is not more machinery or better, not new organizations, or more and novel methods, but men whom the Holy Spirit can use, men of prayer, men mighty in prayer. The Holy Spirit does not flow through methods, but through men. He does not come on machinery, but on men. He does not anoint plans, but men - men of prayer." [20]

Chapter Twelve: PRAYER AT THE MASTER'S LEVEL

"Now my heart is troubled, and what shall I say? 'Father, save me from this hour?' No, it was for this very reason that I came to this hour. Father, glorify your name!" (John 12:27-28 NIV)

Prayer That Trusts

Jill Briscoe once told a remarkable story about her son, David. As a young child, he was scheduled to have an x-ray on Monday morning, so his dad told him about it Friday afternoon. He reminded David that he wouldn't have school on Monday, but had an appointment for his x-ray.

When Monday came, David climbed into the car and sat there white as a sheet. His dad questioned him, "David, you're not scared, are you?"

"Of course I'm scared, Dad ... *I know what an execution is!*" [21]

Amazing. This child, who had pondered his gruesome fate all weekend, still trusted his dad enough to get into the car and go. He must've known dad would work it out somehow.

That kind of unflinching trust in God vibrates at the core of all mature prayer lives. It showcases an advanced level of prayer. Notice how Jesus himself prayed with genius at that Master's level of prayer.

Jesus had recently raised Lazarus from the dead, so witnesses spread the news all over Jerusalem, a city now full of Jews and proselytes who'd traveled from throughout the world for the Feast. When he entered the city in triumph, the crowds mobbed him with unabashed enthusiasm, but the Pharisees said, "See, this is getting us nowhere. Look how the whole world has gone after him!" (John 12:19 NIV)

About that time a group of Greeks who'd come for the Feast asked Philip if they could see Jesus.

With the request of these Gentile proselytes, it was now clear. Jesus had developed a worldwide appeal, even among other nations. But his unprecedented popularity signed his death warrant among the Pharisees. They'd soon take steps to have him executed.

This rip-tide of popularity on the one hand and the plotting of his enemies on the other put Jesus' prayer life to the ultimate test.

His ministry had been so successful that it made Israel tingle. He healed the sick, raised the dead, comforted the despised, fed the hungry and fascinated his listeners with details about the kingdom of God. His ministry had reached a God-ordained zenith of popularity.

Most preachers would consider such success and worldwide popularity a sign their glory days had arrived. Jesus didn't. Something else had to be done.

He told his disciples, "I tell you the truth, unless a kernel of wheat falls to the ground and dies, it remains only a single seed. But if it dies, it produces many seeds. The man who loves his life will lose it, while the man who hates his life in this world will keep it for eternal life." (John 12:24-25 NIV).

To finish his mission, Jesus had to die. He had to "plant the seed" and let it germinate. As the only perfect man, the only one to flawlessly obey God, he had to submit to death.

All other men deserve the death sentence, the one Adam got as he exited the Garden of Eden, but not Jesus. He would submit to death as a substitute, a volunteer on behalf of all Adam's sinful kin.

Prayer That Suffers

Imagine what he's facing. The very crowd that now carries him on a cresting wave of popularity will soon be howling for him to die. One of his own would betray him. His closest friends will deny they even know him.

Have you ever been betrayed by a friend? Or a relative? Have you ever been slandered by people you trusted? Have you ever been accused of something you didn't do? Have you ever been wrongly punished? How did you feel?

Have you ever been ashamed? Ever disappointed someone who believed in you? Ever been caught in sin and felt a stinging guilt? Have you ever felt that brutal, crushing shame, the kind that whispers "you'd be better off dead"?

How would you feel if all your secret sins were published in the media?

How would it feel to be held accountable for *all the sins of another person...* maybe a thief, a rapist, a child-molester, or even a murderer? How would it feel to stand under the guilt of all the evil people alive today... *of all the evil done by the human race... past, present and future!?*

That kind of psychological and spiritual torture would drive any of us insane (some people have killed themselves over the guilt of just one act). Yet Jesus volunteered to *take it all on himself.*

He stood under the Divine wrath and suffered complete separation from his Father. He suffered an eternal hell on that cross in about six hours. He marched into hell for a heavenly cause - *you.*

Prayer That Obeys

It was because of us. It was for our sake that he soberly evaluated his prayer life, asking heart-piercing questions about it:

"And now my heart is troubled." Jesus, the Son of God, wasn't made of steel. The horror and dilemma of what he now faced forced him into a gut-wrenching decision.

"And what shall I say? 'Father save me from this hour?'" That's certainly one possibility. He could have changed his mind and called those legions of angels. He could have let us suffer the hell we deserve. He didn't *have to* save us.

So what would his prayer be? Would it be a self-preservation prayer, a "save me from this hour" prayer?

"No, it was for this very reason I came to this hour. Father, glorify your name!"

Maybe this is the very reason *we've* come to this hour. Maybe the Father expects us to ditch all our "save me from this hour" prayers and start praying with some maturity. Maybe then we can pray for his name to be glorified and his will to be done on earth as it is in heaven.

When you learn to pray that way you're praying at the Master's level. Your prayer life takes giant leaps forward. You plant the seed and it dies, which allows the Father to cultivate the plant and produce the fruit.

The problem with such spiritual growth is that it feels like death. It feels like you're being driven to an execution instead of an x-ray.

Don't let that stop you. Trust in the Father; he knows what he's doing. Let the selfish little kernel of wheat die and watch how God transforms it into a booming harvest.

That's prayer as Jesus prayed it, prayer at the Master's level.

Chapter Thirteen: LOVE ON ITS KNEES

❄

"Simon, Simon, Satan has asked to sift you like wheat. But I have prayed for you, Simon, that your faith will not fail." (Luke 22:31-32 NIV)

When Royalty Kneels

The Baroness Blixen, whose life the movie "Out Of Africa" dramatized, stood politely fidgeting in the receiving line waiting to greet the new Governor of Kenya.

His VIP reception, which featured all the area's prominent socialites, dragged on with bland predictability. But what the Baroness was planning to do ... well, nobody could've predicted that.

Changing times hadn't been kind to her. She once owned a massive coffee plantation, including tribal lands of the Kikuyu people, but lost it during the financial bust following World War I.

Certainly that loss stung her, but what really burned was the new owners' attitude; they planned to throw the Kikuyu off their ancestral lands.

And this once-wealthy aristocrat had no money to buy back the land. She had no political clout and she found no sympathy when trying to work through government channels to help the Kikuyu.

Distraught, discredited and broke, she now saw the new Governor's reception as a last chance, a shoestring tackle to save the people she loved. As the receiving line crept ahead slowly, she saw her opening.

The Baroness collapsed to her knees right in front of the Governor and began begging him to save the Kikuyu. Shocked onlookers tried to pull her away, but it was too late. She had ditched a lifetime of social correctness and "prayed" for the people who owned her heart.

She begged the Governor, "Please look into this matter! Please give me your word!" At that, the Governor's wife stood. "You have *my* word," she said. [22]

Like a rose growing in a garbage dump, Baroness Blixen's selfless love glistened in contrast to the empty social phoniness of her time. She really cared.

That quality - *caring* - is the golden heart of intercession; truly *love on its knees*.

When God Kneels

Jesus' intercessions for Peter glow as a classic example of love on its knees. While Peter daydreamed of being a hero, Jesus saw disaster ahead for this fisherman's faith.

"Simon, Simon, Satan has asked to sift you like wheat." (Luke 22:31 NIV)

Peter knew what that meant. He'd seen wheat sifted, often. He knew how farmers hitched up oxen to a massive sled studded with metal teeth on the bottom. He'd seen oxen waiting as bundles of cut wheat were thrown on the stone floor. And he remembered the sound, the floor groaning, popping and squeaking under the sled's crushing weight.

He knew it was a violent process; the grinding pressure attacking the wheat until little was left. And Peter knew that what was left then went to the sieves; workers pitched the grain and residue into the air, letting the wind separate the wheat from the chaff.

Don't you think a cold chill crawled up Peter's backbone when he realized what Jesus meant?

Peter knew he was about to be reduced to this lowest. What would be left? Anything of value? He, like Job, crouched in Satan's crosshairs waiting for the hammer to fall. If Peter had an ulcer, it was throbbing now.

Notice how Jesus reassured him. "But I have prayed for you, Simon, that your faith may not fail." Notice he said, "I *have* prayed." He didn't wait for the crisis to hit, but prayed long before it came. Being a master at spiritual warfare, Jesus knew to aggressively go on the offensive before Satan could strike a blow.

And notice that he prayed for Peter's *faith*; he didn't pray for Peter to escape trial, but to come out of it intact.

So Jesus committed himself to pray for the people he loved. He had often interceded for Peter, even though the fisherman never knew it. Jesus prayed for him (who probably had prayed little himself) because Peter hadn't understood the ruthlessness of the dark demonic army now glaring at him.

Does It Work?

Did Jesus' hours of intercession do Peter any good? At first you might not think so. Peter failed Jesus. There's no glossing over it. He and the other disciples evacuated when Jesus needed them. Peter cursed and denied he even *knew* Jesus.

Satan probably laughed while he wrote Peter off. A typical dime-a-dozen fisherman. Crushed down to his basic elements. Sifted. Just as Satan thought, nothing there. Only a common coward. He'd certainly pose no threat to Satan's plans.

But something invisible silently continued to bubble. Those hours of prayer for Peter just wouldn't die. They smoldered like embers in a dead campfire; you think it's out, and then it roars back to life and chars a whole forest.

Peter roared back to life on Pentecost. He stood and stared at the same people he once feared. He stood and boldly preached, without slacking, about

Jesus to the very people who had yelled "Crucify him!"

The coward had now become a crusader, the wimp a warrior. Due to Jesus' tireless prayers for a flawed fisherman, history shook to its foundations. The church age began, the Holy Spirit came and 3,000 new Christians were born in one morning.

Yes, it really works. Intercession always betters the situation ... *always*.

Then why aren't we using it more? Instead of verbally roasting people who disagree with us, why not pray for them?

Instead of having "roasted preacher," "baked pastor," "bar-b-qued song leader" and "grilled church member" for Sunday lunch, why not *intercede* for them?

Aren't there people around you needing prayer? Maybe a confused teenager, an uncaring spouse, an ineffective preacher, a faithless elder, a divided congregation, a hurting church member?

As someone once put it, "Is it because we pray so little, that we criticize so much?"

Why criticize? *Satan may be sifting these people like wheat*. So why not pray for them that their faith won't fail?

When Love Prays Through

For years Joe's mom watched him sell drugs and become more entangled in organized crime. Her heart broke while he served time in jail, again and again. But she didn't give up. She prayed. Sometimes he'd arrive home to find her kneeling, interceding for his soul.

One day Joe, searching for something to read in a prison garbage can, found a tract from a church prison ministry. He wiped off the food. He read it. When he called the phone number, someone came. Joe became a Christian and has since become a preacher and won hundreds to Jesus.

On a TV interview several years ago, Joe was asked why. Why had God so changed him?

Do you know what Joe credited as a major factor in his new life? You guessed it, his mother's tireless prayers.

Intercession. The silent, golden ministry. Love on its knees. *You're never more Christ-like than when you pray for others.*

Chapter Fourteen: THE GREAT INTERCESSION

"After Jesus said this, he looked toward heaven and prayed…." (John 17:1 NIV)

Prayer Near The End

Alfred Nobel got a rude shock one morning.

The Swedish chemist opened his daily newspaper and saw his own obituary! It said:

"Alfred Nobel, the inventor of dynamite, who died yesterday, devised a way for more people to be killed in war than ever before, and he died a very rich man."

Actually, it was Alfred's older brother who had died, but reporters grabbed the wrong obituary. Their mistake changed Alfred's life. And it changed history. When the bungled obituary horrified Nobel, he realized he'd be remembered only as the man who invented dynamite, a tool for mass human destruction. His horror motivated him to establish the Nobel Prize, awards still given today to outstanding scientists, writers and peace activists.

Nobel said, "Every man ought to have the chance to correct his epitaph in midstream and write a new one."

Life sometimes gives you the chilling chance to stare at your own obituary: you hear bad news from a doctor or that truck barely misses you on the highway or you see old people at your high school reunion. Nothing clears the mind like facing your own mortality. The trivial things burn off and only the essentials remain. Life comes into sharp focus.

Even Jesus, when facing the end of his earthly work, focused with laser-like intensity on the mission ahead ... not only his mission, but the future of his disciples. He knew he'd have to leave them behind to carry out his work.

In his great intercession, often called the most powerful prayer ever prayed, Jesus shows again the towering presence of his petitions.

Prayer For Himself

"Father, the time has come. Glorify your son" (John 17:1 NIV).

Jesus' first request might seem strange. He asks to be *glorified*. Why? Is it pride? Isn't this selfish request beneath the dignity of Jesus' usual approach?

To understand his prayer, think of what led up to it.

During the Passover meal he had gotten up from the table, wrapped a towel around himself, taken a basin of water and had begun to wash the disciples' feet. He wanted them to see how far his love would go (John 13).

Then Jesus told them it was time for him to leave this earth, but he consoled them by explaining that he would send the Holy Spirit as their mentor.

Finally, in John chapter 17, Jesus prayed aloud for these disciples and their turbulent future. His first request? "Glorify your son." Why? Because they won't have a chance against Satan *until Jesus is glorified*.

Being glorified; what will it mean? It'll prove that Jesus fulfilled his (and man's) destiny. It'll liberate humanity from Satan's dictatorship. It will put mankind in the ascendancy over Satan for the *first time since Adam and Eve abdicated*. It'll mean that the Holy Spirit can come to the infant church's aid with supernatural power... "Up to that time the Spirit had not been given, since Jesus had not yet been glorified." (John 7:39 NIV)

Being glorified; it will *forever reverse the degraded condition of the whole human race*. Adam's fall brought shame. It brought sin and Satan's oppressive rule. But Jesus brought life and immortality to light through the gospel.

Jesus, the Last Adam, placed himself between hell and the whole race. In Jesus, God became man and picked up the fallen battle flag that once flew as a symbol of man's rule over the creation, the flag that fell along with Adam and Eve. Jesus took that flag and raised it again, and was glorified ... *on our behalf!* (Hebrews 2:5-18).

So Jesus' prayer for glorification isn't silly self-ishness. It's the same prayer he taught his disciples earlier: "Hallowed be your name, your kingdom come, your will be done." As always, the Father's will was Jesus' prime request. And it's the Father's will that one man be glorified on our behalf.

Should *we* pray to be glorified also? You bet! Paul wrote that, in God's eyes, we're *already* glorified, by his grace (Romans 8:30). In the Father's mind, we've *already* been raised to sit with Jesus in the heavenly realm; this allows him to "show us off" to angels and the dark supernatural world. He proves to them that He, not Satan, is truly God and deserves worship (Ephesians 2:6-10).

So, by Christ's unselfish work, we share in his position. When he was glorified, so were we. His prayer, "Glorify your son," made our glorious destiny a reality.

Prayer For His Disciples

After praying for his own place in the Father's will, Jesus passionately prayed for his disciples:

"I pray for them ... protect them by the power of your name ... so they may be one ... My prayer is not that you take them out of the world but that you protect them from the evil one." (John 17:11, 15 NIV)

As Jesus prayed this he knew Satan as a formidable enemy, a Commander in Chief ruling hordes of evil supernatural creatures. He'd seen the devil nose-to-nose and defeated him in hand-to-hand spiritual combat.

Jesus also knew that, after his resurrection, an embarrassed and defeated Satan would counter-assault, using all his destructive power against the new born church. The remedy? Attack the devil's dark kingdom with a preemptive strike ... by *prayer*.

That was *always* Jesus' tactic. For example, he prepared himself for forty days with fasting (and obviously prayer) before confronting Satan in the wilderness (Matthew 4:1-2). He taught his disciples to pray, "Deliver us from the evil one." He even rebuked Satan's thoughts when they came through Peter's voice: "Get behind me, Satan!" (Matthew 16:23 NIV) He prayed for Peter when Satan wanted to sift him like wheat (Luke 22:31-32).

Jesus not only taught his disciples a healthy respect for Satan's devious power, but he taught them the remedy ... *prayer*.

So in John 17, Jesus *prayed* for them to be spared from Satan's wickedness. Like the Good Shepherd who's concerned about predators taking his sheep, Jesus prayed down the Father's divine protection on this band of helpless disciples.

He also prayed for them to be set apart for a holy life: "Sanctify them by the truth" (John 17:17 NIV). He *prayed* for them to be set apart for the battle, to become seasoned warriors, to be men of faith and holiness. *It comes by prayer*.

So don't miss the point. Think soberly while you look over Jesus' shoulder and overhear this majestic prayer. Don't forget, he's in the last hours of his life on earth. He faces horror and agony beyond our ability to grasp. He will taste bitter alienation from his own Father and his divine homeland. On top of that, he'll transfer the destiny of his work in the hands of these flawed, human disciples.

At this critical hour, Jesus resorts to the most powerful spiritual weapon he knows. The one that'll stop Satan in his tracks. The one that paralyzes the evil one, ripping apart his kingdom. The one that hedges the disciples in and protects them from supernatural counter-assault. The one we often neglect, thinking it to be primarily powerless... *prayer*.

Prayer For Us

In the next phase of his prayer, Jesus intercedes for future generations of believers: "I pray also for those who will believe in me through their message." (John 17:20 NIV)

What he asks for is sobering, and pivotal to the church's future. The answer to Jesus' prayer will buttress two awesome foundations of his church's existence: (1) the world will believe that the Father actually sent Jesus, and (2) the church will understand that the Father loves *us* as much as he *loves Jesus*.

All those realizations will rest on this evidence: the church is *one*: "That all of them may be one, Father, just as you are in me and I am in you." (John 17:21 NIV)

This idea, which is supposed to win the world and uplift the church, still gives us trouble. We know the church isn't truly unified, yet Jesus prayed for it. Was his prayer too optimistic? Has it gone unanswered for two thousand years? Will the church *ever* be one?

Actually, the church is *already* one! The Father answered Jesus' prayer by making us one in the Spirit: "Make every effort to keep the unity of the Spirit through the bond of peace." (Ephesians 4:3 NIV)

Notice he said "keep" the unity. You can't keep something you don't already have. The church already has unity of the Spirit, our job is to keep it healthy with a "peace bond", a determination to make Jesus proud of us by the way we treat each other.

And it helps to understand what Jesus *didn't* pray for. He didn't pray for (nor expect) total unanimity of opinion. (Even Paul and Barnabus had a sharp dispute over mission methods in Acts 15:39.)

And Jesus didn't pray for total doctrinal agreement (look at Romans 14). But he did pray for the church to be *one* as he and the Father are *one*... spiritually. That oneness means that the Father's love, which was in Jesus, "may be in them and that I myself may be in them." (John 17:26 NIV)

So, while we'll never see unanimity of opinion or doctrine this side of heaven, we can experience oneness of spirit in the church. We can experience a love that astounds and attracts the earthlings around us. How? By *prayer*.

Continued Prayer For Us

That's why Jesus spent his last few pre-resurrection hours praying for all his disciples to live in (and pray for) unity. He knew it meant survival for the family.

Several years ago *National Geographic* published a telling incident about the importance of unity. Several arctic musk-oxen came under attack by a pack of wolves. To protect the young calves, eleven adult musk-oxen circled together with their heads inside the circle and their hooves forming the outer perimeter. This left the wolves nothing to attack but the sharp hooves and powerful legs of the musk-oxen.

But the wolves persisted. As they howled and snarled, one musk-ox finally broke ranks and ran. Some of the others panicked and soon the whole group was vulnerable. As the adults scattered, none of the calves survived. [23]

That's why Jesus prayed so hard for our unity in the Spirit. In the last hours of his life on earth, he prayed passionately for the Father to do three things: glorify his son, protect us from Satan, and give us a spirit of oneness in love.

We can pray the same. We *must*. Don't wait to read your obituary in the paper. Capture the future for God by praying as Jesus prayed.

Chapter Fifteen: PRAYER'S FINEST HOUR

"Father, if you are willing, take this cup from me; yet not my will, but yours be done."
(Luke 22:42 NIV)

The Problem Of Trust

Several years ago National Public Radio aired this revealing story:

Back in the 1950's a Boeing 707 became the first plane to use jet engines in commercial aviation. Not long after the 707 began flying regular passenger service, two men riding in an old pre-jet DC-6 began discussing the fantastic new jet engines.

As they talked of this great aviation news, one of the men mentioned that he worked as a Boeing engineer; the other man excitedly begged for all the inside info about the jet engine's development.

The Boeing engineer proudly told of his company's testing process and their long experience with engines - from the B-17 to the B-52.

"Have you flown on the new 707?" the traveler asked.

"No, I think I'll wait until it's been in service for a while." [24]

Trust. Even when you're on the inside track and know all the information, it's hard to trust.

Trust means risk. It means evaluating, thinking, assessing ... but then putting your whole weight down on something (or someone), thereby giving up control.

It's like the old story of daredevil Jean Francois Grandet, known as Blondin, who performed on a tightrope strung across Niagara Falls.

In 1859 he went across on a bicycle, pushed a wheelbarrow, turned somersaults, pushed a small stove to the middle where he cooked an egg, had a man below the falls shoot at a hat which Blondin held out as a target, walked across on stilts and even walked the tightrope at night, extinguishing a light half way across and proceeding in the dark.

But just when the crowd thought he couldn't top himself, Blondin made a startling announcement: he would carry a volunteer across on his shoulders!

He looked at the crowd and asked, "How many of you think I can walk across with a man on my shoulders?" Most of the spectators raised their hands in agreement.

"Who'd like to be first?" he asked.

No takers. Despite all they'd seen him do, no one wanted to take the risk and trust Blondin's ability. The daredevil persisted until he made his manager do it, but his poor passenger shook so violently that Blondin vowed to never try that stunt again. [25]

Trust means risk, sometimes with danger grinning at you. And trust means relying on someone whose ability surpasses yours, even though the danger and risk intimidate you.

Trust, for the Christian, means the highest grade of spiritual maturity. A selfless, fleshless trust in God becomes a twin to the serious prayer life. Prayer and trust are dance partners in the Divine waltz; they move together and complement each other's grace.

Gethsemane And Trust

Drawing nearer to his humiliating death, Jesus' mind came under withering attack from Satan. Superhuman, supernatural pressure now circled Jesus' prayer life. Would it hold? Would it be a proven and tried weapon?

I once read of an entire British regiment which was lost in battle against the French because of defective weapons; the British swords were made from inferior metal which bent in the crisis of battle. The cost-cutting of an unscrupulous manufacturer ended up costing lives.

Would Jesus' weapon, his prayer life, bend in the coming supernatural warfare? Could it be trusted? His prayer life had, so far, changed the world. But now it would be terribly tested.

As Jesus neared the Mount of Olives and the Garden of Gethsemane that midnight, he told his disciples, "My soul is overwhelmed with sorrow to the point of death." (Mark 14:34 NIV).

That's why he had led them there. His soul now operated at the limits of what the human personality can stand. Satanic pressure surrounded him, pulling him toward a black hole of supernatural evil. With this cosmic battle between God and Satan swirling to a climax, Jesus set himself to *pray*.

Luke's account says that Jesus went out "as usual" to the Mount of Olives (22:39), which echoes what he'd earlier written about Jesus' habit of going to this mountain each night to pray (21:37).

Jesus, the Divine embodiment of a man of prayer, begins by warning his disciples: "Pray that you will not fall into temptation." (Luke 22:40 NIV)

Because their darkest hour now bared its fangs at this little flock, Jesus warned them to pray. Because they stood at the confusing intersection of human destiny, because the spiritual war which began in Eden now entered its most decisive battle, this night's prayer-battle could win or lose it all.

They needed prayer more than they needed to breathe. *Adam's whole race* needed them to pray. And because their prayers would've made Jesus' sufferings more bearable, *he* needed them to pray. Everything in creation groaned, begging them to pray.

But they slept.

When he came back and caught them sleeping, Jesus said "Could you men not keep watch with me for one hour?" (Matthew 26:40 NIV)

It's a little daunting to think about, but Jesus considered a one hour prayer a *short* one. Walking back to where they were, it surprised him that they couldn't even pray an hour.

And the same thing happened each time he left to pray; he came back to find them asleep. While he warred with supernatural forces, fighting valiantly to save us all, his church napped.

Obviously they were exhausted, discouraged, puzzled and full of sorrow. Things weren't going well. Their vision of a glorious kingdom (including themselves as respected cabinet members) wasn't panning out. They could smell death in the air. They could already taste the bitter pill of a lost cause.

But what better time to pray? If that doesn't describe a ripe situation for prayer, nothing does. Jesus thought so. He prayed until he sweat blood. But they slept.

How expensive was their nap? When the crisis hit, Peter denied that he even knew Jesus. At the time, it seemed the only thing to do. But later, when his eyes met Jesus' piercing stare, Peter cried bitterly. Those haunting eyes, deeply set in pain, kept looking at him. I'm sure it took Peter a lifetime to overcome that one… *if he had only prayed.*

But the others fared no better. Matthew later wrote, "All the disciples deserted him and fled" (Matthew 26:54 NIV). (How tough was it for Matthew to put *that* one on paper?)

And then there was Judas. Instead of praying, he plotted; he missed the prayer session that night, but soon arrived sheepishly leading the mob which would arrest Jesus.

Due to their prayerlessness, no one was ready except Jesus. He alone faced the devil's invasion, with no help from his hapless, prayer-less disciples. *Nothing puts us at odds with Jesus' mission faster than prayerlessness.*

The Prayer Of Release

While the church slept, unwilling to sacrifice too much, Jesus released himself in an act of undeniable trust. The aftershocks of his Gethsemane prayers still touch broken people even today.

On a bleak night in an olive garden, Jesus prayed with such intensity that bloody sweat rolled from his face and dripped into the soil. With his face to the ground, he begged his Father with "strong crying and tears to the one who could save him from death, and he was heard because of his reverent submission." (Hebrews 5:7 NIV)

He asked, "Father, if you are willing, take this cup from me; yet not my will, but yours be done." (Luke 22:42 NIV)

Like the snow-topped peaks of the Himalayas, some prayers jut far above all the rest. Their majesty towers high into the spiritual atmosphere, dwarfing all the selfish praying we do in the lowlands.

Moses prayed one of those breath-taking prayers; you can still see its peak today. He said to Jehovah,

"But now, please forgive their sin — but if not, then blot me out of the book you have written." (Exodus 32:32 NIV) He was willing to die for, or with, those people if it would help.

Next to that peak, you can still see one prayed by Paul: "For I could wish that I myself were cursed and cut off from Christ for the sake of my brothers, those of my own race, the people of Israel." (Romans 9:3-4 NIV)

Even though these two prayers rise high into the spiritual atmosphere, the one prayed by Jesus still towers above all else. His prayer stands at a new level, a higher plane. His prayer transcends the need to shape God's agenda to man's. It makes an historic transition; it doesn't cry out for God to yield to human will, but pours itself into the shape of God's will. It asks to be clay on the potter's wheel so that God, not man, can be glorified through the human drama.

Such prayer surpasses the first two levels: (1) prayer for one's own needs and (2) prayer for the needs of other people; it reaches to the third heaven, the most-noble level, asking, "What does *God* want?"

With that, you have the purest, highest goal of all prayer: ultimate trust, that hungering to be shaped to fit God's will, not to conform Him to yours.

When your prayer life orbits around that goal, breakthrough is inevitable. A new energy will fuel your discipleship. You'll operate from a base of spiritual health, not fear.

Most of the remarkable breakthroughs I've seen came after hungering for God's will. Our church has often been transformed because we prayed, "Lord, this is *your* church, not ours. Do with us as you please."

When you pray like that, you open up a Divine dynamic which most people never experience. Trust is prayer's finest hour.

When Florence Nightingale turned thirty years old she wrote this: "Now no more childish things, no more vain things. Now, Lord, let me think only of thy will."

At the end of her life, after years of unselfish service in nursing, someone asked her for the secret to her remarkable story. She said, "Well, I can only give one explanation. That is, I have kept nothing back from God." [26]

Jesus showed us prayer's finest hour; he kept nothing back from God.

Chapter Sixteen: PRAYERS FROM THE CROSS

"Jesus said, 'Father, forgive them, for they do not know what they are doing.'" (Luke 23:34 NIV)

The Terror Of The Cross

The "house of a thousand terrors" stood on a corner of the marketplace in Rotterdam, Holland.

During the 16th century, when King Philip II of Spain sent his army into Rotterdam to crush a revolt, soldiers went house to house slaughtering anyone trapped in their homes.

Several people hiding in a corner house could hear the screams from down their street. And they could hear the soldiers coming closer.

Quickly, one of the trapped men rushed out behind the corner house and brought in a goat. Dragging it to the front hallway, he slit its throat. The others jumped into action, grabbing brooms and sweeping blood under the door. When a squad of soldiers arrived to batter down the door, their leader shouted, "Come away, the work is already done ... look at the blood!" [27]

When Jesus' blood cascaded down that cross, the work was done. He stood under the terror of that torture, removing the terror from our future.

He paid the ultimate price in body, soul and spirit; in body, because his flesh was shredded by man's most inhumane capital punishment on the cross, and in soul and spirit, because he went to hell on that cross.

In six hours his Divine spirit could suffer all the horrors of hell without ever leaving the cross. Whether he went to hell as a location or not (he told the thief that they'd be in Paradise that very day), hell certainly rushed upward to meet *him*, served up right there in his cruel predicament.

I've heard it said that the nails didn't hold Jesus on the cross, *love* did. I'm sure that's true. Love held him on the cross, but *prayer empowered him while he was there*.

We know that, because he prayed several prayers from the cross. And one of the most remarkable was this one: "Father, forgive them, for they do not know what they are doing." (Luke 23:34 NIV)

Jesus' remarkable prayer life can't be understood without grasping what he was doing in this prayer. And your prayer life can't be cultivated unless you model it.

"Father, Forgive Them"

Robert Schuller once told this amazing story about forgiveness. In his California church, Schuller had a close family friend named Bernice. One day at church Bernice called him aside with a complaint. She noticed in the church announcements that a Kamikaze pilot would speak next week. Was it true? A Kamikaze pilot here?

Yes, said Schuller, it was true; the pilot had trained as a Kamikaze, but the war ended just before he flew any missions. He had since become a Christian and had a fantastic testimony about his changed life.

Just then, Schuller winced as he remembered. Bernice's son had been killed in World War II by a Kamikaze.

Bernice told Schuller she just couldn't handle it. She couldn't come next Sunday. Too many painful memories. Too much bitterness.

That next Sunday the Kamikaze spoke. He told of his conversion to Christ. He wept. They all wept together.

But on his way out of the building, as he was walking up the aisle with Robert Schuller and greeting the crowd, Bernice surprisingly confronted him. She stepped from her pew into the aisle and said, "My son was killed in the war by a Kamikaze!"

Schuller and the others held their collective breath. What would she say to the human product of the system that had killed her child?

She drew herself up and said, "God has forgiven you for your sins ... and tonight He has forgiven me of mine." [28]

Forgiveness. It's one of those mysterious keys to the deeper life.

Unforgiveness doesn't look like much of a hurdle, but it kills more prayer lives than we can number. Jesus himself said it. During one's prayers, unforgiveness can tear the whole process apart (Mark 11:22-26). He even included it in his Model Prayer (Luke 11:4).

And Jesus practiced his own preaching. On the cross, in such heart-breaking agony, he asked the Father to forgive the very people who were torturing him. Jesus couldn't have prayed that "Father, forgive them" prayer if he *himself* hadn't already forgiven them.

God Forgave

Have you ever thought about it? After Jesus prayed this prayer, it was answered! Not just in the general sense of God forgiving humanity, but in the specifics, in the living, breathing lives of these same people who had names, families, jobs and friends. How do we know the forgiveness was that specific?

Think about what happened after Jesus' resurrection. When Peter preached the first gospel sermon he told the crowd that God made this same Jesus "whom you crucified" both Lord and Christ (Acts 2:36). These were the very same people, the howling lynch mob that had yelled, "Crucify him!" These same people now stood listening to Peter's sermon. They had screamed for God's death; they wanted to kill the Son himself, to snuff out the Divine spirit in Jesus.

And yet, *in answer to Jesus' prayer*, God offers them forgiveness through Peter's sermon. And *three thousand* of them accept it (Acts 2:41). They found rescue from God's wrath through Jesus' prayer from the cross.

So do we. And so do others, when we grow up spiritually and pray "Father, forgive them", no matter what they've done to us.

As Charles Spurgeon once said, "Let us go to Calvary to learn how we may be forgiven. And then let us linger there to learn how to forgive." [29]

There we learn that forgiveness doesn't excuse evil. It doesn't condone depravity by saying, "What they did to me was all right." Forgiveness means letting go of any claim to judge and punish the offender, leaving justice in God's hands. As a friend of mine says, unforgiveness is like taking poison and hoping the other person will die.

So, following Jesus' lead, the Apostle Paul once wrote, "Do not take revenge, my friends, but leave room for God's wrath, for it is written, 'It is mine to avenge; I will repay, says the Lord.'" (Romans 12:19 NIV)

Praying for one's enemies while forgiving them rises to the level of a Christ-like intercession.

Prayer Of The Forsaken

Jesus' next prayer from the cross is the most chilling, and the most confusing. According to Matthew's account, he prayed "My God, My God why have you forsaken me?"

Why would Jesus pray that? Is he taking back everything he ever taught about faith, courage and trust? Doesn't this prayer seem like the cry of a man who's giving in to the evil, a man who sees that his optimistic dreams have been crushed?

Is Jesus' cry of agony from the cross an admission of his ministry's failure? No, it's actually the *fulfillment* of his ministry.

His prayer from the cross is tightly linked to Psalm 22. No, Jesus isn't quoting poetry while on the cross. He isn't quoting Psalm 22, he's *living* it. Read the Psalm. It's interlaced with the crucifixion account, and he's living out the agony of the man pictured in Psalm 22.

Jesus now tastes estrangement from God (something he never experienced before). He now knows by experience the terror of Adam's rebellion and banishment from the Garden of Eden. He identifies with Cain, who said "My punishment is more than I can bear ... I will be hidden from your presence." (Genesis 4:13-14 NIV).

Even though Jesus had no evil in him, he hung on that cross and was made "to be sin for us, so that we might become the righteousness of God." (2 Corinthians 5:21 NIV) Therefore, he put himself in the same place as every other innocent man tortured by his enemies. He became one with every sufferer.

He's one with the woman abused by a violent husband, or with the child who dies painfully. He's one with the woman who's raped and killed by a stranger, with the lonely widow who loses her home to crooked speculators, with the prisoner falsely accused, with the man cheated out of his life's savings, with the person who's lynched by a racist mob, with the child who cries out from a concentration camp.

You see, God so loved us that he wasn't afraid to come here and wear the rags of the forsaken. He suffers with us, so he can take our suffering and make something eternally beautiful out of it.

As the forsaken man overwhelmed by evil, Jesus prays the prayer of the forsaken.

Some people blame God when they feel forsaken. They say, "If God is so powerful and so loving, why doesn't he do something about all this evil and suffering?" They assume that God is watching all this suffering from his cosmic easy chair.

But one look at the cross, and this prayer from the cross, makes a lie out of that idea. God cares. *Evil hurts God as much as it hurts you*. He joins you in the suffering. That allows him to be there in it ... to be there for you. To strengthen you during the suffering, he's willing to crawl inside it with you, like a mom curling up in bed with her fevered child, willing to take the risk of infection.

So Jesus isn't really asking for information when he prays, "why?" He already knows why. His prayer is, at its core, the cry of the forsaken. A cry we all take up at some point in life. When it happens, you see this prayer in a clearer light.

And so Jesus, having forgiven his murderers and having cried out with the forsaken, now prays a last prayer, one of trust and commitment.

"I Commit My Spirit"

Again, one of Jesus' prayers from the cross uses a Psalm as its backdrop. Jesus the Jewish Rabbi prays the Psalter as he'd done hundreds of times before, but now he *lives it* with deepening agony.

"Into your hands I commit my spirit; redeem me, O LORD, the God of truth" King David writes in Psalm 31:5.

Like Psalm 22, this psalm laments the forsaken man, the sufferer barely hanging on, the outcast who cries to God for refuge. At root, his final leap toward rescue is summed up, *"Into your hands I commit my spirit."*

With this same prayer, Jesus breathes his last. It is finished. The suffering is almost done. He now totally commits himself and his future to the Father, to the one who was always the center of his focus, the hub of the spiritual wheel. He casts himself, without looking back, on the character and oath of his Father.

That's the ultimate, highest level of prayer.

To be totally committed to the Father, to seek holiness, to walk as he walked no matter what the consequences ... that's the ultimate prayer experience.

As your prayer life grows gradually from the *self*-oriented to the *God*-oriented, you experience a Father-and-child walk with God that thrills you more than any single, spectacular answer to prayer.

Jesus knew that experience. It was normal for him; he wants it to be normal for us.

Prayer From Your Cross

Hearing Jesus pray from the cross stirs something deep inside us. Hearing him pray charts a course, sets a goal, motivates a longing to pray more like that. But you can't pray like that and still ride a recliner. If you want to pray like a crucified man, you'll have to climb upon a cross.

Maybe that's why Jesus said, "If anyone would come after me, he must deny himself and take up his cross daily and follow me." (Luke 9:23 NIV)

The cross dominated the central destiny of Jesus' earthly ministry, and he knew a cruciform life would also purify us... and purify our prayer lives, too.

A person being crucified doesn't worry too much about money, taxes, political solutions, popularity, fashion, etc. He's too busy dealing with dying. He's too busy facing eternity. He's too busy praying.

Cross-shaped prayers cut through the religious noise and the Sunday morning hype. Prayers from the cross do three things: they (1) forgive those who need it, (2) identify with the forsaken and (3) commit one's spirit fully to God.

Try praying cross-shaped prayers. It'll change your life and rock the world around you. Just like Jesus.

Chapter Seventeen:
THE DISASTER OF PRAYERLESSNESS

"You do not have because you do not ask God." **(James 4:2 NIV)**

Tying God's Hands

I once read about a young native preacher who, thanks to a wealthy benefactor, flew back and forth monthly from his remote town to the capitol city for his theological training. When the flight attendants would offer him soft drinks and snacks, he'd always decline with a polite "No, thanks."

Finally, on his last trip home at the end of his schooling, the preacher was prepared. When the flight attendant offered her usual snacks he reached into his pocket, taking out the money he'd saved for the occasion. Surprised, she said "Oh, sir, snacks are *included* in the price of your ticket."

Now that you've seen Jesus' prayer life in action, can you see how much you've been missing because you haven't truly understood prayer? What benefits keep escaping you because you've pushed prayer to the back burner or cut it adrift in a sea of confusion?

Is it possible that you've tied God's hands by prayerlessness?

Is it even *possible* to tie God's hands? Can God be limited by human behavior? Are there some things even *God* can't do?

Yes. For one thing, he can't lie. The Bible says it's not just unlikely - but impossible! (Hebrews 6:18.) He *can't do it.*

And here's another thing God can't do... *force* someone to become a Christian. The gospel works only when teamed up with human will. Since he created us in his image (with free will like his,) he can't take over a human life without that person's consent.

And another thing... he *can't answer prayers that aren't prayed.* He doesn't act unless we ask.

That's why God didn't:

- Save Jacob from Esau until he *asked* (Genesis 33:4).
- Free Israel from Egypt until they *prayed* (Exodus 2:23).
- Forgive Israel's sin until Moses *interceded* (Exodus 32:14).

- Give Hannah a child until she *prayed* (1 Samuel 1:20).
- Spare Jerusalem from Assyria until King Hezekiah *asked* (2 Kings 19).
- Strengthen Jesus in Gethsemane until he *prayed* (Luke 22:43-44).

Do you see the point? God works in answer to prayer; when prayers are absent, God waits. James put it this way: "You do not have because you do not ask God." (James 4:2 NIV)

Prayerlessness Is Hazardous

How serious is this issue? Well, did you know that the Babylonian Empire once invaded Jerusalem because God's people *wouldn't pray?* It's right there in Ezekiel's writings; the Jews went to Babylon as prisoners of war for over seventy years *due to prayerlessness.*

Note the astounding statement God made: "I looked for a man among them who would build up the wall and stand before me in the gap on behalf of the land so I would not have to destroy it, but I found none, so I will pour out my wrath..." (Ezekiel 22:30-31 NIV)

Did you catch that? "*Stand before me* in the gap *on behalf of the land*" - that's prayer! God plainly said that he had to destroy Jerusalem for her sins because *no one prayed.* The seemingly simple sin of prayerlessness trapped them in an ancient holocaust at the hands of Babylon.

Prayerlessness & Disaster

And Ezekiel's day wasn't the only time when disaster rode into town on the back of prayerlessness. Look at the other times in Scripture *when life turned tragic due to lack of prayer*:

(1) The Gibeonite tribe fooled Joshua into thinking they came from a distant country when they actually lived only three days away. Believing he was safe, Joshua made a treaty with them (against God's will). Then, because of his sworn oath not to destroy them, Joshua was stuck babysitting a pagan tribe living in his promised land; he even had to go to war to protect them (Joshua 10:6).

How did it happen? Joshua and his men had investigated the Gibeonites' claims by looking over their provisions, but "did not inquire of the LORD"... they didn't *pray first*. (Joshua 9:14 NIV)

(2) Here's another one. When Samuel confronted Israel about their sin of asking for a king to replace Jehovah, he reminded them of their prayer-history. During Israel's slavery in Egypt, "they cried to the LORD for help". And later in their suffering during the time of Judges, "they cried out to the LORD".

But in contrast, in Samuel's day, when in trouble they cry, "we want a king to rule over us." Instead of praying, they ask for a *political solution*.

When he warns them of their tragic mistake, the Israelites beg Samuel to pray for them.

He answers, "As for me, far be it from me that I should sin against the LORD by failing to pray for you." (1 Samuel 12:23 NIV) Samuel considered their prayerlessness a *sin*.

(3) One king named Ahaziah even *died* from prayerlessness. He had fallen through the lattice of his upper room and injured himself, but instead of praying to Jehovah he sent messengers to consult Baal-Zebub, a pagan god. Because of that, he died (2 Kings 1:1-17).

(4) Prayerlessness ended King Saul's reign. After his suicide, the Bible says he died because he was unfaithful to Jehovah... "and did not inquire of the LORD." (2 Chronicles 10:13-14 NIV)

(5) As King David ordered the Ark of the Covenant moved into Jerusalem, a worker named Uzzah mishandled the Ark and fell dead. The Ark couldn't be moved for over three months because they didn't ask God how *he* wanted it transported.

Later when King David mounted a new effort to take God's Ark into Jerusalem, he explained why they failed the first time: "We did not inquire of him (God) about how to do it in the prescribed way." (1 Chronicles 15:18 NIV)

(6) King Asa ended the last years of his reign in prayerless disgrace because he "relied on the King of Aram and not on the LORD." He died with a painful disease because "even in his illness he did not seek help from the LORD, but only from the physicians." (2 Chronicles 16:7-12 NIV)

(7) When Jesus' own disciples failed to cast a powerful demon out of a young boy, they asked, "Why couldn't we drive it out?" Jesus said, "This kind can come out only by prayer and fasting." (Mark 9:29 NIV) Jesus had just *prayed all night* on the mount of transfiguration, but they hadn't prayed so they had little power.

(8) When Jesus prayed in the Garden of Gethsemane, he told his disciples to "Watch and pray so that you will not fall into temptation." (Mark 14:38 NIV) They didn't pray, so they fell. They all scattered, denying Jesus with curses.

(9) And later, after his resurrection, Jesus sent word to the seven churches of Asia. He said that one of them made him sick, the *most sickening church in the Bible*. Because of their lukewarm attitude he intended to spit them out. Why were they so sickening?

Jesus exposed their prayerlessness: "You say, 'I am rich; I have acquired wealth and do not need a thing.'" (Revelation 3:17 NIV) Their pride in personal achievement left no room for prayer, which resulted in apathy, which *sickened* Jesus.

By now the evidence is clear; *one of the saddest tragedies to overtake God's people is prayerlessness...* especially when you realize that our *intimacy with God has been paid for* as part of the *ticket price of salvation!*

But Why?

After studying the subject for a while it begins to sink in; *prayerlessness hinders God's work and ties his hands.* But why?

Why is God hindered by our prayerlessness? Why can't God work in spite of prayerless people; why can't he just work around us? Is it *really* true that God can't work without praying humans?

Why doesn't God work unless we pray?

Chapter Eighteen: WHY GOD DOESN'T ACT UNLESS WE ASK

"For our struggle is not against flesh and blood... Therefore put on the whole armor of God... and pray in the Spirit on all occasions with all kinds of prayers and requests."
(Ephesians 6:12-18 NIV)

The Heart Of Prayer

It seemed like a normal day at the auto dealership. A man dropped by the Delaware car lot to look at vehicles and soon found a truck he wanted to test drive. When he identified himself as a local firefighter, the staff allowed him to take the pickup for a spin. But the spin turned into a tour... and then into a hijacking. The man never returned.

The State Troopers who were called found out right away that the test driver wasn't a firefighter after all, so they activated the stolen truck's electronic locator system. Its signal soon led cops right to the truck and to the thief, who was also caught with illegal drugs.

Does that electronic beacon remind you of something… maybe of prayer? That's what it reminds me of, and here's why.

Our world has been hijacked by evil. When God created this world, he did it perfectly. And he created man to have dominion over it. But then Satan, the pretender, came on the scene and stole the entire world from man, who was the rightful owner. Now Satan has the whole world hijacked to his control and he operates as "god of this age." (1 John 5:19 & 2 Corinthians 4:4)

Despite that, the beacon of prayer keeps on pulsing. Mankind's prayers keep sending out the alert that something's wrong.

But why do we need to keep sending out the beacon of prayer? Doesn't God realize that we're in trouble?

I used to wonder about that. Why should I pray? If God knows all things, and he cares and he knows what to do, why do I need to pray?

Here's the answer as it unfolds in a cosmic three-act drama:

Act One: God Created The World For Us

Obviously, God created the world. Genesis knows no other explanation. Neither do the Psalms. In Psalm eight, David praises God for his majestic creation:

"When I consider your heavens, the work of your fingers, the moon and the stars, which you have set in place, what is man that you are mindful of him, the son of man that you care for him?" (Psalm 8:3-4 NIV)

So, God created the universe. It's his. David calls it "*Your* heavens, the work of *your* fingers" - God owns it all, right? But look at the rest of David s song.

"You made him (man) ruler over the works of your hands; you put everything under his feet..." (Psalm 8:6 NIV)

What an astounding concept! God created the world, but then *gave it to man*. He gave it to us and made us "rulers" over it. God created it, which means he could give it away to anyone he wished.

And the language of the first chapters of Genesis agrees:

"Then God said, 'Let us make man in our image, in our likeness, and let them rule over the fish of the sea and the birds of the air, over the livestock, over all the earth...'" (1:26 NIV)

"God blessed them and said... 'Rule over the fish of the sea and the birds of the air...'" (1:28 NIV)

Even if you stopped reading the Bible right there, you'd come away with two basic concepts: (1) God created man in the Divine image (with a sovereign will) and (2) God created a perfect world, giving it to man as a gift.

But then the trouble started.

Act Two: Man Gave It Away

Satan entered man's perfect world and began a psychological war to invade humanity's dominion and wrestle it from his control.

And the soldiers in Satan's mental assault were his words: "Is it true? I mean, did I hear you say that you can't eat of *any* of these beautiful trees? What a shame. All this beautiful garden and you can't even enjoy it."

Eve answered, "Oh, no. We can enjoy it *all*. God gave it to us... But, now that you mention it... there is *one* tree we can't have. But God said we couldn't eat from that one because we'll know both good *and* evil. That tree's poison; if we eat from it we'll die."

Having planted a seed of doubt, the serpent pressed the attack. "Die!? You won't *die* if you eat from that one! Haven't you heard? *That* tree actually does the opposite. It makes you think like God."

Eve gave in. She ate. She gave it to Adam and he ate.

Now that they'd both taken what belonged to God, the hedge protecting them from evil rotted away. Having committed high treason, they became partners with Satan, signing up for life-sentences in the devil's dark kingdom.

When Satan stole their hearts, he also hijacked the creation. He replaced man as lord of the earth.

And Satan took office right away. Not only was the creation now hostile to man (food came only by sweat, and childbirth by great pain), but a black hole opened and sucked man's moral, family and social world into the pit. The first human family became profoundly dysfunctional, watching in horror as one brother murdered the other.

And it grew worse. Satan's grip intensified. By Job's day Satan openly confronted God about the ownership of man's heart. Satan eagerly wanted to test Job: (Does Job *really* love God, or is it just a ploy to maintain his blessings... doesn't he actually have more kinship with Satan than with God?)

Although God still stood between Satan and Job, the Devil's argument was, and is, powerful: *man is actually on Satan's turf, not God's.* The prototype Man in Eden had ejected God from his heart. He opted for Satan's control. So if God then puts a hedge around Job, which protects him from the devil, isn't that unfair competition?

God relents. He allows Satan to test Job. God knows that Satan is partly right.

So the Book of Job pictures Satan ruthlessly holding on to the territory he gained in the Garden of Eden. And in Job's story the devil's control over earth even extends to creating storms, crime, death and illness.

By New Testament times, Satan had carved out some titles for himself: "prince of this world" (John

12:31, 14:30 & 16:11 NIV) and "god of this age" (2 Corinthians 4:4 NIV).

When he tempted Jesus in the wilderness, Satan showed him all the world's kingdoms and said, "I will give you all their authority and splendor, for it has been given to me, and I can give it to anyone I want to. So if you worship me, it will all be yours." (Luke 4:6-7 NIV)

Notice that Jesus refused to worship Satan, but he didn't argue with his premise. He knew that Satan ruled in most human hearts and minds, especially those of the politically powerful.

So, by the end of the New Testament, John writes: "the whole world is under the control of the evil one." (1 John 5:19 NIV)

Therefore the whole world, man's mental, social, moral, political and economic world, lies under Satan's control.

Until you understand that Satan rules Adam's kin today, *prayer won't be an urgent priority*. You'll assume that everything that happens is *automatically* the will of God. You won't understand why prayer is so crucial. Until you know that we're behind enemy lines, you won't pray without ceasing.

Act Three: Jesus Came To Reclaim

Now that this world had fallen under Satan's lordship, neither God nor man could exercise complete dominion over man's world. But then God's answer arrived.

It took a "last Adam" to *undo* what the "first Adam" did (1 Corinthians 15:45.) Since man gave dominion of the world over to Satan, a man (one of the same specie) would have to win it back.

That's where Messiah enters the picture. Throughout the Old Testament, God promised a remedy to Satan's treason. And it wasn't a program, an institution or a new set of laws. The remedy was a *Person*.

He would be the Anointed One, a God-Man powerful enough to recapture what Adam had given away.

Because Jesus was God-in-flesh (John 1:1-14), *he stood where Adam once stood* and rejected Satan's offer. He was "tempted in every way, just as we are - yet was without sin." (Hebrews 4:15 NIV)

Jesus did it for man... *as a man*; "the reason the Son of God appeared was to destroy the devil's work." (1 John 3:8 NIV)

Jesus' work established a new beachhead (the "Kingdom of God") in the war to win mankind back to God. The Kingdom is a new race, new species of man, "new creation," a new kind of human who's *in Christ* instead of *in Adam*.

By his work Christ has *now reestablished man as head over the creation*. He sits as a human being enthroned at the Father's right hand. He's there in a resurrected, glorified human body. He represents us. Mankind, in Christ, is *back where God intended him to be!* Even the "world to come" won't be controlled by angels, but by mankind (Hebrews 2:5-18). Man will even rule over angels (1 Corinthians 6:2-3). *In*

Christ, man will have complete victory over what Satan did to God's creation.

Right now we don't see man ruling, but we see Jesus. He's been tried, crucified, resurrected and glorified... as one of *us*. He rules in our place and on our behalf. Like the men who went to the moon in 1969. Only one man stepped on the surface, but *mankind* went to the moon.

Now that a man rules, Satan has fallen from his authority in the heavens (Revelation 12:7-10). Mankind, *in Christ,* is back on the throne and in the process of a counter-attack against Satan's dominion.

That's what the Kingdom of God is about, continuing Jesus' mission of destroying the devil's work. We're behind enemy lines. We're the Marines on the beachhead. We attack and counter-attack the evil one's kingdom *by prayer and the ministry of the word* (Acts 6:4).

Our job is to finish Messiah's work. He's given us the power and authority to raid and loot Satan's kingdom (Matthew 28:18-20). He expects us to regain dominion over evil; in Christ we have the power to accomplish it! But it can't be done without mastering the weapon of intense prayer.

Therefore, We Pray

God won't force down any doors. He won't force anyone to be saved. He won't force anyone to love him because he respects human freedom of will.

Are there times when God just works from sovereign choice, without being asked? Possibly so, but the Bible never gives us the luxury of sitting around passively prayer-less while God does our part for us. Therefore, we pray.

Prayer invites God back into the process. It invites him back into the human heart and the human condition. It honors him by asking him to work, to be directly involved in the daily drama.

While Adam's kin has pushed God away, the praying person asks God to return to active involvement in the cosmic drama on the human scene. That's why Jesus carried on an almost continuous conversation with his Father as he "often withdrew to lonely places and prayed." (Luke 5:16 NIV)

The Bible is literally packed with such stories, proving that God doesn't work unless we ask. Understanding all this, *how can we remain prayerless?*

Chapter Nineteen: WHY GOD WAITS

"Come to me, all you who are weary and burdened, and I will give you rest." (**Matthew 11:28 NIV**)

Use your imagination.

As you sit reading this, you feel a gentle hand on your shoulder. A little startled, you look around and gaze straight into the face of an *angel*.

"The Lord Jesus will see you now."

As you sit in shock, he says again, "The Lord Jesus will see you now. He's waiting in the next room." With that, he points toward the room and motions for you to follow.

How could this be happening? Is it a dream... a vision? As you try to think it through, you move toward the room and see a glow coming from under the door. You touch the knob and feel a tingling vibration. You cautiously open the door… and there stands *Jesus*!

He's not what you expected. He isn't the wimpy, bloodless caricature you've seen in medieval paintings. He's *real*. He's the healthiest, most powerful person you've ever met.

And his eyes rivet you. The love radiating from those eyes captures you… it fills the whole room and vibrates the walls. The love is so intense, so magnetic that you don't want to ever leave.

Just then Jesus surprises you by stepping forward and embracing you. As he enfolds you in the warmest, most reassuring hug you've ever felt, he says, "I *love* you."

He continues, "You don't know how much we love you, more than all else we've created. The Father and I eagerly wait for the day that you'll come and live with us forever."

As he talks, you see the healed wounds where the nails pierced him. You melt. You now know beyond a doubt that he loves you. And that he always will.

But you feel so inferior to him, so shamed by your sins. Yet you know that he understands… that he accepts you anyway. He's seen you at your worst, but he still loves you. Knowing all about you, he's still willing to embrace you.

As he steps back to smile at you again, he says, "I just wanted us to have this time together. I don't hear from you much anymore. Have I done something to offend you? Or is it something that *you've* done and are feeling guilty about?"

What would you say? What's been keeping you from an ecstatic, passionate walk with him as your soul-mate? Someone you need to forgive? Something you need to confess?

As your heart breaks, you pour it out on him. He listens. He understands. He wants to heal the wounds you've suffered in hand-to-hand combat with the devil.

As you pour it out on him you protest, "Lord, I'm so sorry. I just don't give you all that you deserve from me!"

With that, he says, "I don't want what you can do for me... I want *you*."

That's the heart of prayer.

God waits for you to pray because he waits for *you*. You are his joy, his reason for coming here, his reason for answering prayer.

Prayer is family time with your Father. It's sitting in the family room and talking to the God of all creation... your Father.

God waits for you to pray. God waits for *you*. God waits...

Appendix One

THE PRAYER LIFE OF JESUS IN THE GOSPELS

- Prayer at His Baptism – Luke 3:21
- Prayer for Direction In His Ministry – Mark 1:35
- His Commitment to Prayer Despite Time Pressures – Luke 5:16
- Prayer when Making Major Decisions – Luke 6:12
- Prayer and Power to Produce Miracles – Matthew 14:23
- Prayer for Open Hearts and Receptive Minds – Luke 9:18
- Prayer and His Transfiguration – Luke 9:28-29
- His Habit of Prayer and Praise – Luke 10:21 (Matthew 11:25-26)
- His Prayer Life Stirs the Disciples – Luke 11:1-13

- Praying for the Children – Matthew 19:13-14
- Prayer That Raised the Dead – John 11:41-42
- Prayer as Planting the Seed – John 12:27-28
- His Habit of Thanksgiving in Prayer – Matthew 14:19; 26:26-27 (Mark 6:41; 8:6-7; 14:22-23; Luke 9:16; 22:17-19)
- His Prayers of Intercession – Luke 22:31-32
- His Great Intercessory Prayer – John 17:1-26
- Jesus' Prayers in the Garden – Luke 22:39-46
- His Prayers from the Cross – Luke 23:34, 46

Appendix Two

WHAT JESUS TAUGHT ABOUT PRAYER

- Prayer for One's Enemies – Matthew 5:43-44 (Luke 6:27-28)
- Sincerity in Prayer – Matthew 6:5-8
- The Model Prayer – Matthew 6:9-15 (Luke 11:1-4)
- Persistence in Prayer – Matthew 7:7-12 (Luke 11:5-13)
- Praying for Evangelistic Harvest – Matthew 9:35-38 (Luke 10:1-2)
- Prayer and Unity – Matthew 18:18-20
- His People to be a House of Prayer – Matthew 21:12-13 (Mark 11:15-17; Luke 19:45-46)
- Persistence in Praying for Justice – Luke 18:1-8
- Prayer and the Right Heart – Luke 18:9-14
- Prayer and Spiritual Warfare – Mark 9:28-29

- Praying in Faith – Mark 11:20-25 (Matthew 21:18-22)
- Hypocritical Prayers – Mark 12:40 (Luke 20:47)
- Prayer in Crisis Times – Matthew 24:20-21 (Mark 13:18)
- Prayer in Jesus' Name – John 14:13-14; 15:7&16; 16:23-27
- Prayer and Intercession – Luke 22:31-34

Appendix Three

FORTY DAYS WITH THE BIBLE'S GREAT PRAYERS

1. ABRAHAM'S PRAYER FOR SODOM - Genesis 18:20-33.
2. JACOB'S PRAYER FOR MERCY FROM ESAU - Genesis 32:6-12.
3. MOSES' PRAYER AT THE BURNING BUSH - Exodus 3:1 – 4:18.
4. MOSES' PRAISE AFTER THE RED SEA CROSSING - Exodus 15:1-18.
5. MOSES' FIRST PRAYER FOR ISRAEL'S SIN - Exodus 32:7-14.
6. MOSES' SECOND PRAYER FOR ISRAEL'S SIN - Exodus 32:30-34.
7. MOSES' PRAYER FOR GOD'S PRESENCE - Exodus 33:12 – 34:9.

8.   MOSES' 40-DAY PRAYER - Deuteronomy 9:18-20 & 9:25-29.

9.   JOSHUA'S PRAYER TO STOP THE SUN - Joshua 10:12-13.

10. HANNAH'S PRAYER FOR A CHILD - 1 Samuel 1:1-20.

11. DAVID'S PRAYER OF PRAISE FOR GOD'S KINGDOM - 2 Samuel 7:18-29.

12. SOLOMON'S PRAYER FOR WISDOM - 1 Kings 3:4-15 (2 Chron. 1:5-12).

13. SOLOMON'S PRAYER TO DEDICATE THE TEMPLE - 1 Kings 8:22-61.

14. HEZEKIAH'S PRAYER FOR DELIVERANCE - 2 Kings 19:14-19.

15. HEZEKIAH'S PRAYER FOR HEALING - 2 Kings 20:1-6.

16. JEHOSHAPHAT'S PRAYER IN A CRISIS - 2 Chronicles 20:1-23.

17. NEHEMIAH'S PRAYER FOR JERUSALEM'S PLIGHT - Nehemiah 1:3-11.

18. DAVID'S PRAYER OF PRAISE - Psalm 8.

19. DAVID'S PRAYER FOR A PURE HEART - Psalm 19.

20. DAVID'S PRAYER TO HIS SHEPHERD - Psalm 23.

21. DAVID'S PRAYER FOR FORGIVENESS - Psalm 51.

22. DAVID'S PRAYER FOR GUIDANCE - Psalm 139.

23. ISAIAH'S PRAYER FOR MERCY - Isaiah 64:1-12.

24. JEREMIAH'S PRAISE OF GOD'S WISDOM - Jeremiah 32:17-27.

25. DANIEL'S PRAYER OF CONFESSION - Daniel 9:4-19.

26. JESUS PRAYS AT HIS BAPTISM - Luke 3:21-22

27. THE MODEL PRAYER - Matthew 6:9-15.

28. JESUS' HABITS OF PRAYER - Luke 5:15-16 & 9:18.

29. JESUS' ALL NIGHT PRAYER BEFORE CHOOSING THE TWELVE - Luke 6:12-13

30. JESUS' ALL NIGHT PRAYER AT HIS TRANSFIGURATION - Luke 9:28-29

31. JESUS' PRAYER OF PRAISE - Matthew 11:25-26 (Lk. 10:2 1)

32. JESUS' ALL NIGHT PRAYER ON THE MOUNTAIN - Matthew 14:13, 23-27 (Mk. 6:46)

33. A PRAYER THAT RAISED THE DEAD - John 11:41-42

34. JESUS' PRAYER FOR HIS DISCIPLES - John 17.

35. JESUS PRAYS FOR WEAK DISCIPLES - Luke 22:31

36. JESUS PRAYS IN GETHSEMANE - Matthew 26:36-44 (Mk. 14:32f & Lk. 22:39f)

37. JESUS' PRAYERS FROM THE CROSS
    - Matthew 27:46 (Mk. 15:34) Luke 23:46;
    Luke 23:34
38. THE CHURCH'S PRAYER FOR
    BOLDNESS - Acts 4:23-31.
39. PAUL'S PRAYERS FOR THE
    EPHESIAN CHURCH - Ephesians 1:15-
    23 & 3:14-21.
40. PRAYERS OF WORSHIP IN HEAVEN
    - Revelation 11:15-19; 15:1-4; 16:5-7.

NOTES:

1. Craig Brian Larson, *Illustrations for Teaching and Preaching* (Grand Rapids: Baker, 1993) # 169.
2. Paul Lee Tan, *Encyclopedia of 7700 Illustrations* (Rockville, MD: Assurance, 1979) #6547.
3. Ibid, #4637.
4. Craig Brian Larson, *Illustrations for Teaching and Preaching* (Grand Rapids: Baker, 1993) # 223.
5. Paul Lee Tan, *Encyclopedia of 7700 Illustrations* (Rockville, MD: Assurance, 1979) #5132.
6. J.W. McGarvey, *Commentary on Matthew and Mark* (Delight, AR: Gospel Light, 1875 reprint.) Page 132.
7. Paul Lee Tan, *Encyclopedia of 7700 Illustrations* (Rockville, MD: Assurance, 1979) #4805.

8. Ibid, #4806.
9. Craig Brian Larson, *Illustrations for Teaching and Preaching* (Grand Rapids: Baker, 1993) # 65.
10. Jack Canfield & Mark Victor Hansen, *Chicken Soup for the Soul* (Deerfield Beach, FL: Health Communications, 1993) Page 228.
11. Ibid, Page 229.
12. William J. and Randy Petersen, *100 Amazing Answers to Prayer* (Grand Rapids: Fleming H. Revell, 2003) Page 68.
13. Albert M. Wells, *Inspiring Quotations Contemporary and Classical* (Nashville: Thomas Nelson, 1988) #2124.
14. Craig Brian Larson, *Illustrations for Teaching and Preaching* (Grand Rapids: Baker, 1993) # 55.
15. John Bisagno, *The Power of Positive Praying* (Grand Rapids: Zondervan, 1965) Page 24.
16. Dick Eastman, *The Hour That Changes The World* (Grand Rapids: Baker, 1986) Page 25.
17. E.M. Bounds, *Power Through Prayer* (Chicago: Moody, 1980 reprint) Pages 54-59.
18. Ibid, Page 53.
19. Craig Brian Larson, *Illustrations for Teaching and Preaching* (Grand Rapids: Baker, 1993) # 221.

20. E.M. Bounds, *Power Through Prayer* (Chicago: Moody, 1980 reprint) Page 10.

21. Jill Briscoe, *In The Father's Arms* (Carol Stream, IL: Christianity Today, 1995) Preaching Today tape #141.

22. Dr. Douglas Kelley, *Perseverance In Prayer* (Jackson, MS: RTS Ministry Magazine Vol. 10, #2, Summer 1991) Page 8.

23. Craig Brian Larson, *Illustrations for Teaching and Preaching* (Grand Rapids: Baker, 1993) # 254

24. Craig Brian Larson, *Illustrations for Teaching and Preaching* (Grand Rapids: Baker, 1993) # 79.

25. Richard B. Manchester, *Incredible Facts* (New York: Bristol Books, 1990) Page 150.

26. Paul Lee Tan, *Encyclopedia of 7700 Illustrations* (Rockville, MD: Assurance, 1979) #825.

27. Ibid, # 483.

28. Robert Schuller, *The Be Happy Attitudes* (Waco, TX: Word, 1985) Page 144.

29. Albert M. Wells, *Inspiring Quotations Contemporary and Classical* (Nashville: Thomas Nelson, 1988) # 917.

CPSIA information can be obtained at www.ICGtesting.com
Printed in the USA
LVOW130246050412

276270LV00001B/50/A